University of Nebraska
Lincoln, Nebraska

Written by Aaron Eske

Edited by Kimberly Moore
and Jon Skindzier

Layout by Jaime Myers

Additional contributions by Omid Gohari,
Christina Koshzow, Chris Mason, Joey Rahimi,
and Luke Skurman

ISBN # 1-4274-0182-9
ISSN # 1552-1443
© Copyright 2006 College Prowler
All Rights Reserved
Printed in the U.S.A.
www.collegeprowler.com

Last updated 05/15/06

Special Thanks To: Babs Carryer, Andy Hannah, LaunchCyte, Tim O'Brien, Bob Sehlinger, Thomas Emerson, Andrew Skurman, Barbara Skurman, Bert Mann, Dave Lehman, Daniel Fayock, Chris Babyak, The Donald H. Jones Center for Entrepreneurship, Terry Slease, Jerry McGinnis, Bill Ecenberger, Idie McGinty, Kyle Russell, Jacque Zaremba, Larry Winderbaum, Roland Allen, Jon Reider, Team Evankovich, Lauren Varacalli, Abu Noaman, Mark Exler, Daniel Steinmeyer, Jared Cohon, Gabriela Oates, David Koegler, Glen Meakem, and the University of Nebraska Bounce-Back Team.

College Prowler®
5001 Baum Blvd.
Suite 750
Pittsburgh, PA 15213

Phone: 1-800-290-2682
Fax: 1-800-772-4972
E-Mail: info@collegeprowler.com
Web Site: www.collegeprowler.com

Welcome to College Prowler®

During the writing of College Prowler's guidebooks, we felt it was critical that our content was unbiased and unaffiliated with any college or university. We think it's important that our readers get honest information and a realistic impression of the student opinions on any campus—that's why if any aspect of a particular school is terrible, we (unlike a campus brochure) intend to publish it. While we do keep an eye out for the occasional extremist—the cheerleader or the cynic—we take pride in letting the students tell it like it is. We strive to create a book that's as representative as possible of each particular campus. Our books cover both the good and the bad, and whether the survey responses point to recurring trends or a variation in opinion, these sentiments are directly and proportionally expressed through our guides.

College Prowler guidebooks are in the hands of students throughout the entire process of their creation. Because you can't make student-written guides without the students, we have students at each campus who help write, randomly survey their peers, edit, layout, and perform accuracy checks on every book that we publish. From the very beginning, student writers gather the most up-to-date stats, facts, and inside information on their colleges. They fill each section with student quotes and summarize the findings in editorial reviews. In addition, each school receives a collection of letter grades (A through F) that reflect student opinion and help to represent contentment, prominence, or satisfaction for each of our 20 specific categories. Just as in grade school, the higher the mark the more content, more prominent, or more satisfied the students are with the particular category.

Once a book is written, additional students serve as editors and check for accuracy even more extensively. Our bounce-back team—a group of randomly selected students who have no involvement with the project—are asked to read over the material in order to help ensure that the book accurately expresses every aspect of the university and its students. This same process is applied to the 200-plus schools College Prowler currently covers. Each book is the result of endless student contributions, hundreds of pages of research and writing, and countless hours of hard work. All of this has led to the creation of a student information network that stretches across the nation to every school that we cover. It's no easy accomplishment, but it's the reason that our guides are such a great resource.

When reading our books and looking at our grades, keep in mind that every college is different and that the students who make up each school are not uniform—as a result, it is important to assess schools on a case-by-case basis. Because it's impossible to summarize an entire school with a single number or description, each book provides a dialogue, not a decision, that's made up of 20 different topics and hundreds of student quotes. In the end, we hope that this guide will serve as a valuable tool in your college selection process. Enjoy!

OMID GOHARI ◯ CHRISTINA KOSHZOW ◯ CHRIS MASON ◯ JOEY RAHIMI ◯ LUKE SKURMAN ◯
The College Prowler Team

Table of Contents

Introduction from the Author

Many people have a preconceived notion of what attending the University of Nebraska must be like. Some don't view the University as a school at all, but rather as one giant football team. Some think that it's nothing more than an overgrown community college. Then, there are others who equate living in Nebraska with living in a foreign land: Siberia or the Sahara Desert often come to mind. To some degree, these assumptions are not altogether untrue. It's not until you actually move into the dorms, attend a lecture, or come home from a campus party that you can fully understand and appreciate the charm of the real Nebraska.

I never thought I'd choose UNL. When I started my college search, I had five schools in mind, and Nebraska was fifth in line. I just didn't want to see people's bored expressions when I told them I was going to Nebraska. And I most certainly didn't feel like wearing a parka on those arctic January mornings.

I toured the other four schools on my list and was impressed, but I scheduled a visit with UNL just in case. During my visit, I was greeted with more smiles, encouragement, and care than any other university I'd toured. I felt comfortable and at home, and suddenly, with a gallant and powerful thrust, Nebraska leapfrogged ahead of the others.

In most rankings (not counting the AP Top 25 Poll), the University of Nebraska is rated about average. What students, professors, and alumni of Nebraska have learned, however, is that these numbers in no way reflect the experiences and memories of UNL—the college they will always call home.

For those of you who haven't been to UNL, I hope this guidebook shows you a side of Nebraska that will change your inaccurate assumptions. Perhaps UNL isn't the right place for you, but as I learned when I was in your position, never close any doors before you know for sure what's inside.

Aaron Eske, Author
University of Nebraska

By the Numbers

General Information

University of Nebraska
14 and R Streets
Lincoln, NE 68588

Control:
Public

Academic Calendar:
Semester

Religious Affiliation:
None

Founded:
1869

Web Site:
www.unl.edu

Main Phone:
(402) 472-7211

Admissions Phone:
(800) 742-8800

Student Body

**Full-Time
Undergraduates:**
15,684

**Part-Time
Undergraduates:**
1,453

Total Male Undergraduates:
9,102

**Total Female
Undergraduates:**
8,035

Admissions

Overall Acceptance Rate:
74%

Total Applicants:
8,871

Total Acceptances:
5,113

Freshman Enrollment:
3,266

Yield (% of admitted students who actually enroll):
64%

Early Decision Available?
No

Early Action Available?
No

Regular Decision Deadline:
May 1

Regular Decision Notification:
Rolling basis

Must-Reply-By Date:
May 1

Transfer Applications Received:
1,622

Transfer Applications Accepted:
1,206

Transfer Students Enrolled:
877

Transfer Application Acceptance Rate:
74%

Common Application Accepted?
No

Supplemental Forms?
No

Admissions E-Mail:
admissions@unl.edu

Admissions Web Site:
http://admissions.unl.edu

SAT I or ACT Required?
Either, ACT more common

First-Year Students Submitting SAT Scores:
17%

SAT I Range (25th–75th Percentile):
1040–1300

SAT I Verbal Range (25th–75th Percentile):
510–640

SAT I Math Range (25th–75th Percentile):
530–660

First-Year Students Submitting ACT Scores:
97%

**ACT Composite Range
(25th–75th Percentile):**
22–28

**ACT English Range
(25th–75th Percentile):**
21-28

**ACT Math Range
(25th–75th Percentile):**
21–28

Freshman Retention Rate:
80%

**Top 10% of
High School Class:**
28%

Application Fee:
$45

Financial Information

In-State Tuition:
$5,540

Out-of-State:
$14,450

Room and Board:
$6,008

Books and Supplies:
$850

**Average Need-Based
Financial Aid Package:**
$7,043

**Students Who Applied
For Financial Aid:**
73%

**Students Who
Received Aid:**
50%

**Financial Aid Forms
Deadline:**
No deadline (priority April 1)

**Scholarship Forms
Deadline:**
January 15

Financial Aid Phone:
(402) 472-2030

Financial Aid Web Site:
www.unl.edu/scholfa

Academics

The Lowdown On...
Academics

Degrees Awarded:
Associate

Bachelor

Master

Doctorate

Most Popular Majors:
22% Business, Management, and Marketing

13% Engineering

10% Education

9% Communication and Journalism

6% Visual and Performing Arts

Undergrad Schools:
Agricultural Sciences and Natural Resources

Architecture

Arts and Sciences

Business Administration

Education and Human Sciences

Engineering

Hixson-Lied College of Fine and Performing Arts

Journalism and Mass Communications

Law

Public Affairs and Community Service (UNO)

Dentistry (UNMC)

Nursing (UNMC)

➜

Full-Time Faculty:
1,022

Faculty with Terminal Degree:
97%

Student-to-Faculty Ratio:
19:1

Average Course Load:
15 credit hours

Class Size:
Fewer than 20 students: 34%
20–49 students: 53%
50 or more students: 14%

Graduation Rate:
Four-Year: 22%
Five-Year: 54%
Six-Year: 61%

Sample Academic Clubs
Advertising Club, Black Law Student Association, Engineers Without Frontiers, Horticulture Club, Nebraska Masquers, Pre-Law Club, Women's Undergraduate Mathematics Network

Special Degree Options
Combined Degree, First Professional, Post-Bachelor Certificate, Post-Master Certificate, Terminal-Associate

AP Test Score Requirements
Possible credit for scores of 3, 4, or 5

IB Test Score Requirements
Possible credit for scores of 5, 6, or 7

Best Places to Study
Love Library, Student Union, Broyhill Fountain

Did You Know?

Three Nobel Prize winners, eight Pulitzer Prize winners, 22 Rhodes Scholars, 18 Goldwater Scholars, and 12 Truman Scholars graduated from the University of Nebraska.

University of Nebraska was the school that famous rockstar **Tommy Lee enrolled at for the NBC reality show**, *Tommy Lee Goes to College.*

Students Speak Out On...
Academics

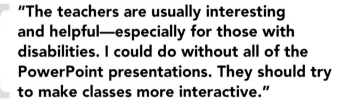

"The teachers are usually interesting and helpful—especially for those with disabilities. I could do without all of the PowerPoint presentations. They should try to make classes more interactive."

Q "I've had mostly positive experiences with professors. But then again, I tried to avoid taking classes from the known awful professors. But overall, mine have been **prepared for class and are willing to work with students**."

Q "The professors are hit and miss—some great ones and others are not so great. The **classes within your major are usually the most interesting**. General requirements can be dull depending on the subject."

Q "Professors are professors. It really depends. They are pretty good, but it depends on your luck. Like any school, **there are good ones and there are bad ones**."

Q "It depends on the subject area. Some are good and **some really suck**."

Q "The teachers at Lincoln are very nice. In the beginning, you will probably have half big classes and half small classes. I have found that even in my big classes the **teachers will try to get to know you individually** and it always helps if you make the extra effort for them to know you."

Q "The teachers here are really, really good. I went to a very good high school, so my college professors had a lot to measure up to, and **I have not been disappointed yet**. I have always had a professor for an instructor and not a TA, which makes a big difference. I was in a big lecture class last semester—probably about 150 kids—and the teacher knew about everyone's names, which is really impressive."

Q "The teachers are hard to group together. Some I liked and some I didn't like. **I don't think anyone has ever been unfair**, though."

Q "They are **some of the best in the country**, if you ask me. Our English department is a prime example of that."

Q "There are going to be good ones and bad ones, and you'll find out the hard way which is which. On the whole, the faculty and staff are great, and I can honestly say I have only had two professors I didn't like (and one got fired). **We get to do student evaluations each semester** to evaluate our teachers, and the administration takes these very seriously. So if you have a problem, tell them. You might have to deal with a bad prof, but you can possibly save someone else from the same fate by relaying information."

Q "For the most part, **I have enjoyed my teachers**, but there are always a few who aren't so great."

Q "Teachers are great, as far as I know. All of mine have been helpful and have pretty good **office hours so that I can come in and see them** if I need help."

Q "All of the teachers that I had this year were very good. **They explained the material very well**. Of course, like on any campus, there are a few bad apples."

The College Prowler Take On...
Academics

According to students, the average UNL professor is just that—average. Some are brilliant and some are wretched, and the rest fit somewhere in-between. If you want to meet a professor who is more than just your average, everyday Joe, then you'll need to take it upon yourself to actually meet them by attending office hours. It's also important to ask your fellow students, or visit *www.pick-a-prof.com* before choosing a course and a professor. Because there are multiple sections for most classes, you often have a choice of instructor, so choose wisely.

You can expect a quality education at UNL. It's not as academically rigorous as the Ivy's, but most students don't choose Nebraska because of its intense academic programs and renowned faculty. Overall, the relaxed coursework (in comparison to the more prestigious private colleges) gives students some extra time to learn outside the classroom. And, yes, there is much more to college than what's in the $120 textbooks.

B-

The College Prowler® Grade on
Academics: B-

A high Academics grade indicates that professors are knowledgeable, accessible, and genuinely interested in their students' welfare. Other factors include class size, how well professors communicate, and whether or not classes are engaging.

Local Atmosphere

The Lowdown On...
Local Atmosphere

Region:
Midwest

City, State:
Lincoln, Nebraska

Setting:
Urban

Distance from Omaha:
1 hour

Distance from Kansas City:
3 hours

Points of Interest:
Historic Haymarket
State Capitol Building

Closest Shopping Malls:
SouthPointe Pavilions
Westfield Gateway

→

Closest Movie Theaters:

Mary Riepma Ross
Media Arts Center

313 N. 13th St.
On campus

(402) 472-5353

http://theross.org

Starship 9 ($2 movies)

1311 Q St
Downtown

(402) 441-0222

www.douglastheatres.com

Lincoln Grand (14-Plex)

12th and P St.
Downtown

(402) 441-0222

www.douglastheatres.com

Major Sports Teams:

Anything Husker

Lincoln Saltdogs (baseball)

Lincoln Stars (hockey)

City Web Sites

www.ci.lincoln.ne.us

www.downtownlincoln.org

Local Slang

Lincoln is literally the center of America, so we tend to borrow slang from all around us. The word "pop" is as common as "soda," and don't worry, no one will laugh at you if you call a couch a sofa.

Did You Know?

5 Fun Facts about Nebraska:

- *Rolling Stone* magazine listed Lincoln as "one of the **best places to hear live music**."
- The State Capitol has been called **the eighth architectural wonder of the world**—it's also been called the penis of the prairie.
- Lincoln's National Museum of Roller Skating houses the **world's largest collection of roller skates** and memorabilia.
- *Sports Illustrated* said Lincolnites are "**some of the friendliest people** on the planet."
- Lincoln boasts **6,000 acres of parkland**—more than any other U.S. city per capita. There are also 60 miles of hiking and biking trails.

Famous People from Nebraska:

311	Henry Fonda
Fred Astaire	Gerald R. Ford
Marlon Brando	James King
William Jennings Bryan	Chris Klein
Buffalo Bill	Malcolm X
Warren Buffet	J. Sterling Morton
Johnny Carson	Nick Nolte
Willa Cather	Alexander Payne
Dick Cavett	John J. Pershing
Guy Chamberlin	Andy Roddick
Dick Cheney	Mari Sandoz
Crazy Horse	Charles Starkweather
Loren Eiseley	James Valentine
Father Flanagan	Daryl Zanuck

Students Speak Out On...
Local Atmosphere

"The town is a basic college town and football is a huge part of it. There is a lot of culture available if you seek it. Stuff to visit: the museums, the Ross, the stadium, coffee shops."

"**There are some fun things in Lincoln**, but it takes work to find them."

"Lincoln is like a big small town. The people are friendly and welcoming. Being a college town, Lincoln is **thriving with young people and social activities**. Visit SouthPointe and the Haymarket."

"It's very much a college town. Many people of the same age group and background live in Lincoln. **I feel very at home in any place around the college** or outside and love the downtown scene. There are very cool people on campus and downtown, but the rest of the town is total suburbia man."

"It's fine, I guess. I'm from Omaha, which isn't exactly a booming metropolis, but nevertheless, moving to Lincoln took some adjustment. There **aren't any interstates through the city, so it takes a little longer to get to where you need to**, but it isn't that big of a deal. I haven't really looked for things to visit in Lincoln, but in Omaha the zoo is awesome and right next door is Rosenblatt Stadium where they hold the College World Series. I love going to that."

Q "It's a good college town with a **combination of large city and small town atmosphere**."

Q "The town has about 230,000 people. There are three other universities and one community college. There are two malls (neither of which are very good). There is **not a lot of stuff to visit**. Omaha is 52 miles away, though, and provides some entertainment."

Q "It is definitely a college town! There is **a state college in the city and another university is not too far**, so many times you will meet people from there at parties."

Q "There is **enough to do to keep busy on a Friday night**, but not really any cool landmarks."

Q "The **entire town revolves around the University**. They are very supportive of the students and athletes. Nothing to stay away from. Nothing in particular to visit either."

The College Prowler Take On...
Local Atmosphere

Judging from students' comments, it's obvious that Lincoln is a college town. There are four colleges in the area, which means there are tens of thousands of college students to run into at bars, sporting events, parties, malls, and concerts. Omaha offers a nice change of pace for when students get tired of the usual Lincoln hangouts.

Lincoln's no NYC, but considering it's 35 times smaller, it still has a enough to keep any young adult occupied. While the city doesn't have a Broadway or any historical landmarks, it does have its share of nature and enough local landmarks to make it feel like home. Lincoln is small enough that, during your senior year, you'll probably recognize someone anywhere you go, but it's also big enough that you're not bored out of your mind after the first week.

The College Prowler® Grade on

Local Atmosphere: B

A high Local Atmosphere grade indicates that the area surrounding campus is safe and scenic. Other factors include nearby attractions, proximity to other schools, and the town's attitude toward students

Safety & Security

The Lowdown On...
Safety & Security

Number of Nebraska Police:
27

Safety Services:
475-RIDE
Blue-light phones
Campus escort
Operation ID

Safety Phone:
(402) 472-3555

Health Center Office Hours:
Monday–Thursday
8 a.m.–6 p.m.,
Friday 8 a.m.–5 p.m.,
Saturday 9 a.m.–12:30 p.m.

Health Services

The University Health Center offers students primary medical care, birth control, counseling and psychological services, dental care, physical therapy, alcohol education, nutrition counseling, weight regulation skills, sexual health information and promotion, smoking cessation, peer education, measles immunization, tuberculosis screening for international students, emergency contraception, counseling and psychological services, dental, radiology

Did You Know?

UNL students get **free psychological consultations at the Health Center**—another way the University takes an interest in the well-being of its students.

Students Speak Out On...
Safety & Security

"I've always felt very safe. I've never heard of anyone I know being assaulted or robbed. There are lots of lights all over the place—very safe."

Q "UNL is a safe campus for the most part. **I always feel very safe** in the daylight and for the most part at night."

Q "**Safety is very good**. I always feel safe, even at night."

Q "I always feel safe on campus. I haven't heard of any problems with that issue thus far. Another service the **University provides is 475-RIDE, which is a free cab** service for anyone who has had a little too much fun."

Q "Security and safety on campus is good. We have a special division of the **Lincoln Police Department on campus patrolling all the time**."

Q "Security and safety are pretty solid. They have **emergency phones all over the campus** as well as campus escorts to walk people home. I can't remember any reports of a major crime on campus since I've been here."

Q "I think safety is very good. Sometimes though, **I think they go a little overboard**."

Q "**I haven't heard of any incidents** on campus all semester."

Q "All-in-all, I think it is very safe. In my three years, I have not heard of any incidents. The only thing is that campus is in a bad part of town. However, Lincoln is not that big, so I don't know what your definition of 'bad' is. All of the **trouble tends to stay in the neighborhoods** and not on campus."

Q "The security is great! I went through my entire first year without ever locking my dorm room door and nothing ever got stolen. I was never afraid to be out at night either. The **campus security officers are excellent**."

The College Prowler Take On...
Safety & Security

UNL students feel overwhelmingly safe on campus. Students mention campus police, blue-lights, 475-RIDE, and campus escort as some of the many safety precautions that help them feel secure. By day, students don't lock their dorm rooms and by night, students traipse through all corners of campus in the dark. Even seniors at UNL say they've never heard of any negative incidents that deserve any undue attention.

Lincoln is a very trusting town and, for the most part, people don't abuse that trust. This is Nebraska we're talking about, and in the "Heartland" people worry more about national football championships, than they do their own personal safety. Don't be too careless, though, unchained bikes do get stolen and there are some shady characters on and around campus from time to time. But on the whole parents, don't be afraid to send your kids here—UNL is an exceptionally safe place for anyone to live.

A

The College Prowler® Grade on
Safety & Security: A

A high grade in Safety & Security means that students generally feel safe, campus police are visible, blue-light phones and escort services are readily available, and safety precautions are not overly necessary.

Computers

The Lowdown On...
Computers

High-Speed Network?
Yes

Wireless Network?
Yes, in most buildings

Number of Labs:
31

Number of Computers:
650

Operating Systems:
Mac OS, Windows

24-Hour Labs:
Yes, in the Student Union and
each residence hall

Free Software

3D Studio Max 2006, Acrobat 7, ADA , Adobe Creative Suite, Adobe Video Collection, ArcView, Arch Desktop 2006, AutoCAD 2006, Avid Xpress, CD-ROM Databases, Final Cut Pro HD, Final Cut Studio HD, Final Draft 7, Government Documents, JAWS, Multimedia Software, Photoshop 7, SPSS 13, Studio MX 2004, ZoomText

Discounted Software

Microsoft Office: $10 (as opposed to $200)

Charge to Print?

If you want laser quality, it'll cost you a dime per page. Otherwise, students get an alotted amount of prints for the old-school dot-matrix printers.

Students Speak Out On...
Computers

{ **"There are plenty of computer labs, some are more crowded than others, but computers are usually accessible. It is very nice to have your own computer, however."**

Q "The computer labs are **always crowded and the printers suck**."

Q "The network is very quick. The labs are almost always open, but **at peak hours they may be full**."

Q "Computer labs are not always crowded, but you should plan accordingly. Useful at night and more crowded during the day. **All the dorms have computer labs**, which are very useful whether you live in them or not."

Q "The computer network is good. **Nebraska has spent a lot of money on updating** their technology. All of the dorm rooms are equipped with an Ethernet connection, so if you want to bring your own computer you can have a really easy, fast connection. The computer labs are not that crowded though, so if you can't bring one, then you'll be fine."

Q "Bringing your own computer is always a plus. The **network is awesome—it's so fast**! However, the labs are never full as far as I can remember, except at peak times."

Q "Usually, the computer labs are not crowded, but I would still recommend bringing your own. It's much more convenient to stay in your room and do your homework. However, it is **definitely not necessary to have one**."

Q "Many people bring their own computers for the sake of convenience. I didn't have my own, so I hung out in the labs. There are computer labs in every dorm complex, in many of the academic buildings and at the Union. They're all **pretty busy during the day**, but if you're like me and stay up until all hours of the night, you'll find the labs to be nearly empty."

Q "I'd **highly suggest bringing your own computer**. The year I lived in the dorms, the labs were always packed. Since then they have added more, but during the busy times of the semester they are still quite full."

Q "One thing that a lot of people do is bring their own computer but not a printer. That way they can type in their rooms and just walk downstairs to the computer lab when they have to print because **all of the paper is free down there**."

Q "I had my own computer and it was really nice, but my roommate did not and she used the computer lab in the dorm. She never had a problem typing a paper or anything. If you just want to check your e-mail, there are **tons of stand-up computers (kiosks) in the dorms** and all over campus. UNL definitely has a really good computer network."

The College Prowler Take On...
Computers

The consensus among UNL students is that the computer labs are up-to-date and normally not crowded—with certain exceptions (finals week, mid-terms). Students recommend bringing your own computer for the sheer convenience, but they also say that life will go on on if you have to use the labs every now and then.

If you're planning on buying a computer, consider a laptop. Most students don't take their laptops to class, but they do come in handy for group meetings and those times you just can't stand to sit idle and listen to your roommate sing the theme song to *Friends* over and over again. Many buildings on campus (such as the Student Union and Love Library) are also wired for wireless Internet, so you can check your e-mail from your very own laptop.

B

The College Prowler® Grade on

Computers: B

A high grade in Computers designates that computer labs are available, the computer network is easily accessible, and the campus' computing technology is up-to-date.

Facilities

The Lowdown On...
Facilities

Student Center:
Nebraska City Union
Nebraska East Union

Athletic Center:
Campus Recreation Center
East Campus Activities
Building

Libraries:
C.Y. Thompson Library
Love Library

Campus Size:
613 acres

Popular Places to Chill:
Broyhill Fountain
Dorm lounges
Student Union

What Is There to Do on Campus?

If you're bored, and homework's the last thing you want to do, you can always swim in Broyhill Fountain, nap in the Student Union, burn some calories at the Rec Center, see a $2 movie across the street at Starship, or stuff your face at the Union Food Court.

Movie Theater on Campus?

Yes, the Mary Riepma Ross Film Theatre shows new independent films daily

Bowling on Campus?

Yes, there are lanes inside the East Campus Student Union

Bar on Campus?

No, but there are plenty just a block away

Coffeehouse on Campus?

Yes, the Caffina Café inside the union serves Starbucks

Favorite Things to Do

As its name suggests, the Student Union is a favorite gathering spot for UNL students. At any given time, hundreds, if not thousands, of students will lollygag the day away by mingling at UNL's main social hub.

Did You Know?

UNL's Architecture Hall is home to **the largest urinal west of the Mississippi**.

Students Speak Out On...
Facilities

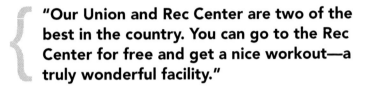

"Our Union and Rec Center are two of the best in the country. You can go to the Rec Center for free and get a nice workout—a truly wonderful facility."

Q "**I freaking love the Union and Rec Center**. They should make classes more available at the Rec, though."

Q "The Rec Center is fantastic—the weight room is incredible. The Student Union is okay, kind of crowded and noisy during the day. The **baseball and football stadiums are amazing**, which makes the sports really fun to watch."

Q "Most of the **facilities are nice, shiny, and clean** like a bald man's head."

Q "The facilities are very clean with a **homey and comfy atmosphere**."

Q "Our Rec Center with a weight room, basketball courts, rock wall, racquetball courts, indoor pool, indoor football field, indoor track, circuit center, and other stuff that I'm forgetting is really brand new. I would give the facilities an **A+—they are really impressive**. Everything is really clean, from locker rooms to all the brand new equipment. There are even saunas in the huge locker rooms."

Q "The Student Union is brand new with **many computers, restaurants, and the bookstore**."

Q "**Everything here is top-of-the-line**—like our baseball field, Memorial Stadium (football), Bob Devaney Sports Center (basketball). All of the facilities are unbelievable. With huge big screens at all of them it's fun because you can see instant replays and everything."

Q "I think Nebraska takes pride not only being number one in sports, but also having **the best conditions to thrive academically**."

Q "The Rec Center is close to the dorms and pretty cool. The computer labs are solid. **The Union may be a bit lacking**."

Q "**We have great facilities**—awesome Rec Center."

Q "The Student Union is beautiful. **It's well-lit and always bustling**."

Q "All of the facilities are good. The **Rec Center is one of the best I have ever seen** and we get free membership to it."

Q "Most facilities are good. **There is room for some improvement**, though. They have made some changes since I've been here, and now it's better."

Q "The athletics are solid, the computers aren't bad (depending on which lab you go to), and the Student Union isn't much (mainly just offices, the food court, and the bookstore). **The Health Center (a.k.a. Death Center) is not very good**. I suggest doing your own diagnosis if you're sick."

The College Prowler Take On...
Facilities

Nebraskans love their Huskers, and they treat both students and student athletes to some breathtaking facilities. Students also gush about the Rec Center, which in the minds of many, leaves nothing to be desired. The Student Union is a popular hangout for many students who enjoy its many amenities and great lighting. Whatever you're looking to do, UNL provides state-of-the-art facilities to accommodate the student body.

Every few decades, UNL enters a new construction phase, one of which is currently underway. In the past few years, no fewer than 18 buildings on campus have either been constructed or completely renovated, which gives campus a very nice traditional-meets-modern feel.

The College Prowler® Grade on

Facilities: A-

A high Facilities grade indicates that the campus is aesthetically pleasing and well-maintained; facilities are state-of-the-art, and libraries are exceptional. Other determining factors include the quality of both athletic and student centers and an abundance of things to do on campus.

Campus Dining

The Lowdown On...
Campus Dining

Freshmen Meal Plan Requirement?

Yes (everyone living in campus housing is required to have one, unless living in Husker or the apartments)

Meal Plan Average Cost:

$2,700 (included in housing contract)

Places to Grab a Bite with Your Meal Plan:

Abel/Sandoz Dining Center

Food: American grill, entrees, vegetarian selection, sandwiches

Location: Abel/Sandoz complex

Favorite Dish: Desserts

(Abel/Sandoz Dining Center, continued)

Hours: Monday–Friday
Breakfast
6:45 a.m.–10:30 a.m.,
Lunch 10:30 a.m.–2 p.m.,
Dinner 4:30 p.m.–7 p.m.,
3:30 p.m.–7 p.m. (Friday);
Saturday–Sunday
Brunch 10:45 a.m.–1:15 p.m.
Dinner 4:30 p.m.–7 p.m.

Cafinna Café

Food: Coffee, tea, smoothies, specialty drinks, baked goods

Location: Nebraska City Union

Favorite Dish: Starbucks

Hours: Monday–Thursday
7 a.m.–8 p.m.,
Friday 7 a.m.–3 p.m.

Cather/Pound/Neihardt Dining Center

Food: Specialty food, traditional fare, Nebraska Dinner Event once a month featuring seasonal and organic products

Location: CPN Complex

Favorite Dish: Chicken strips

Hours: Monday–Friday
Breakfast
6:45 a.m.–10:30 a.m.,
Lunch 10:30 a.m.–2 p.m.,
Monday–Thursday Dinner
3:30 p.m.–7 p.m.

East Union Café and Grill

Food: Made-to-order sandwiches, grill, fruit

Location: East Campus Student Union

Favorite Dish: Cheese fries

Hours: Monday–Friday
Breakfast
6:45 a.m.–9:30 a.m.
Lunch 10:30 a.m.–2 p.m.
Dinner 4:30 p.m.–7 p.m.,
Saturday–Sunday
Brunch 10:45 a.m.–1 p.m.
Dinner 4:30 p.m.–6 p.m.

Food Court

Food: Burger King, Subway, Imperial Palace, Sbarro's, the Bakery

Location: Nebraska City Union

Favorite Dish: Fast food

Hours: Monday–Thursday
9 a.m.–9 p.m.,
Friday 9 a.m.–5 p.m.,
Saturday 11 a.m.–8 p.m.,
Sunday 12 p.m.–8 p.m.

Harper/Schramm/Smith Dining Center

Food: Continental breakfast

Location: HSS Complex

Favorite Dish: Muffins

Hours: Breakfast
6:45 a.m.–10:30 a.m.

Closed for lunch and dinner because of rennovations

The Lounge

Food: Snack bar, mini convenience store

Location: Basement of CPN

Favorite Dish: Snacks

Hours: Sunday–Thursday
7 p.m.–12 a.m.

Selleck Dining Center

Food: Pizza, pasta, deli, soup, ethnic cuisine, American grill, made-to-order omelets, salad bar, frozen yogurt

Location: Selleck Quad

Favorite Dish: Stir-fry bar

Hours: Monday–Friday
Breakfast
6:45 a.m.–10:30 a.m.,
Lunch 10:30 a.m.– 3:30 p.m.,
Dinner 4:30 p.m.–9:30 p.m.;
Saturday–Sunday Brunch
10:45 a.m.–3:30 p.m.,
Dinner 4:30 p.m.–9:30 p.m.

Selleck Express

Food: Pizza, snacks, convenience store

Location: Selleck Quad

Favorite Dish: Pizza

Hours: Daily 8 p.m.–1 a.m.

The Snack Shack

Food: Hoagies, snacks

Location: Abel/Sandoz

Favorite Dish: Smoothies

Hours: Sunday–Thursday
9 p.m.–12:30 a.m.

Village Market

Food: Convenience store

Location: Husker Village

Favorite Dish: Snacks

Hours: Monday–Friday
7 a.m.–1 a.m.
Saturday–Sunday
10 a.m.– 1 a.m.

Off-Campus Places to Use Your Meal Plan:

None

24-Hour On-Campus Eating?

No

Student Favorites:

Food Court

Selleck Dining Center

Other Options

The Hewitt, or the Training Table, is inside Memorial Stadium and is predominantly for student athletes. However, the average Joe student can also eat breakfast and lunch there. The pluses—healthy food including the best fresh fruit and veggies on campus, skinless chicken, and lean red meat. The minuses—hats/bandannas are prohibited and you'll sometimes feel a bit out of place.

Did You Know?

With UNL's meal plan there's **no limit to how many times or how much you can eat in a day**. There are also no limitations to which dining halls you eat in—so if you live in Abel you can still eat with your friends in Smith.

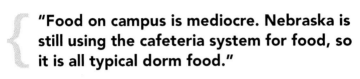

Students Speak Out On...
Campus Dining

> "Food on campus is mediocre. Nebraska is still using the cafeteria system for food, so it is all typical dorm food."

Q "**Dining Hall food gets old by the end of the year**. There are tons of places to eat downtown, though."

Q "Dining halls are mediocre at best. Food in the Student Union is average—**Subway is by far the best restaurant** on campus. There are restaurants near campus, however."

Q "I've never had the cafeteria food, but the **fast-food choices in the Union are good**. There are also many restaurants and food chains within walking distance from campus."

Q "The **dining halls are average**. There are really good restaurants if you look for them—venture out."

Q "The food on campus is fine. My parents must suck in the kitchen because I like the food while others complained. **The desserts are restaurant quality**! All of the dining halls are about the same, except the Training Table, which is far superior in quality compared to the other foods."

Q "The dorms actually served good food. The key was variety and **they serve about six or seven different options at every meal**. In the Student Union, they have the main fast-food restaurants."

Q "I've lived off campus for a couple of years, and the one thing I miss is the food. I know that sounds silly, but it was just so easy. The Student Union has Subway, Burger King, Imperial Palace and some others. There are also a few fast-food places within walking distance of the Union. I think **most of the dorms have snack bars**, too."

Q "In terms of dorm food, **there is definitely something left to be desired**. Fortunately, there are plenty of restaurants close to campus or places that deliver so you won't starve."

Q "Dorm food is good. There are **always a huge variety of things to choose from** so it is hard to not find something you like. There are also snack bars in all of the dorms that open at night if you need a study break or are just hungry. They serve everything from hamburgers and mozzarella sticks to sub sandwiches and ice-cream sundaes. Also, in the Student Union, there is a Sbarros Pizza, an Imperial Palace, a Subway, and a BK."

Q "At the beginning, dorm food is not that bad at all. They actually have some pretty good stuff. If you don't like anything in the line, which I usually didn't unless it was pasta, **they always have a sandwich and salad bar along with soup** and about every kind of cereal you can think of."

Q "The **Hewitt is the dining center under the stadium**. This is where all the athletes eat, but regular students can eat there for breakfast and lunch—it's awesome food."

Q "The on-campus dorm food is not so great, but I don't think it is that great anywhere. I am a vegetarian, and the **vegetarian meals were definitely bad**."

The College Prowler Take On...
Campus Dining

Some students at UNL are more cynical about dorm food than others. The largest complaint is not about the quality of the food, but its repetition. When students can't stomach the idea of nacho bar again, they venture to the Student Union food court or one of many restaurants downtown.

To put it simply, on-campus dining at UNL is not gourmet, but it is low maintenance. If you offered an off-campus student a free meal at a dining hall, he'd jump at the chance because, although it's not spectacular, at least he wouldn't have to shop for it, cook it, or clean up afterwards. But for students who eat dorm food more routinely, some variety sure would sure spice things up.

The College Prowler® Grade on

Campus Dining: C

Our grade on Campus Dining addresses the quality of both school-owned dining halls and independent on-campus restaurants as well as the price, availability, and variety of food.

Off-Campus Dining

The Lowdown On...
Off-Campus Dining

Restaurant Prowler:
Popular Places to Eat!

Amigos Mexican Restaurant
Food: Fast-food Mexican
1407 Q St.
(402) 475-9819
Cool Features: Good greasy food for late-night munchies
Price: $7 and under per person
Hours: Sunday–Thursday 6 a.m.–2:30 a.m., Friday–Saturday 6 a.m. to 3 a.m., Sunday 6 a.m.–2 a.m.

Bison Witches Bar & Deli
Food: Hot sandwiches
1320 P St.
(402) 474-3366
www.bisonwitches.com
Cool Features: The bar/restaurant is always bustling and the sandwiches make your mouth water just thinking about them
Price: $7 and under per person
Hours: Kitchen Daily 11 a.m.–10 p.m., Bar Daily 11 a.m.–1 a.m.

Bruegger's Bagels

Food: Bagels, breakfast

1209 Q St.

(402) 474-6001

www.brueggers.com

Cool Features: They aren't shy when it comes to cream cheese, so savor the generous dollops

Price: $6 and under per person

Hours: Monday–Friday 6 a.m.–4 p.m., Saturday 6 a.m.–2 p.m., Sunday 7 a.m.–2 p.m.

Buffalo Wild Wings (BW3's)

Food: American

1328 P St.

(402) 475-2999

www.buffalowildwings.com

Cool Features: If you're 21 and your friends aren't, you can all hang out at BW3's

Price: $10 and under per person

Hours: Monday 11 a.m.–12 a.m., Tuesday–Saturday 11 a.m.–1 a.m., Sunday 12 p.m.–11 p.m.

Buzzard Billy's

Food: Cajun, creole

247 N. 8th St.

(402) 475-8822

www.buzzardbillys.com

(Buzzard Billy's, continued)

Cool Features: Located in a historic building, large beer selections, birthday club

Price: $15 and under per person

Hours: Sunday–Monday 11 a.m.–9 p.m., Tuesday–Wednesday 11 a.m.–10 p.m., Thursday 11 a.m.–10:30 p.m., Friday–Saturday 11 a.m.–11 p.m.

Chipotle

Food: Burritos, tacos

232 N. 13th St.

(402) 474-1133

www.chipotle.com

Cool Features: These will rival the size of your head, hip atmosphere

Price: $5 and under per person

Hours: Daily 11 a.m.–10 p.m.

Doozy's

Food: Hot sandwiches

101 N. 14th St.

(402) 438-1616

Cool Features: Doozy's heated sandwiches are yummy and can be delivered

Price: $6 and under per person

Hours: Monday–Saturday 11 a.m–9 p.m., Sunday 12 p.m.–7 p.m.

FireWork's

Food: Wood-fired food

210 N. 7th St.

(402) 434-5644

www.telesis-inc.com/ fireworks/index.html

Cool Features: roaring fires and relaxing atmosphere, from-scratch recipes, house brewed ales

Price: $20 and under per person

Hours: Monday–Thursday 4 p.m.–10 p.m., Friday 4 p.m.–11 p.m., Saturday 11 a.m.–11 p.m., Sunday 4 p.m.–10 p.m.

Ivanna Cone

Food: Ice cream

701 P St.
Haymarket

(402) 477-7473

www.ivannacone.com

Cool Features: Homemade ice cream, quirky flavors daily, adorable, perfect place to end a date

Price: $5 and under per person

Hours: Monday–Thursday 12 p.m.–10 p.m., Friday 12 p.m.–11 p.m., Saturday 11 a.m.–11 p.m., Sunday 1 p.m.–10 p.m.

Jimmy John's Gourmet Sandwiches

Food: Sandwiches

101 N. 14th St.

(402) 477-1400

www.jimmyjohns.com

Cool Features: Employees who have more fun at their job than anyone else downtown. They also deliver late into the night

Price: $6 and under per person

Hours: Daily 10:30 a.m.–2 a.m.

Juice Stop

Food: Fruit smoothies

1217 Q St.

(402) 435-4442

www.juice-stop.com

Cool Features: Quick snacks or light and healthy meals, offer about 50 different fruity combinations

Price: $4 and under per person

Hours: Monday–Thursday 6:30 a.m.–9 p.m., Friday 6:30 a.m.–8 p.m., Saturday 8 a.m.–8 p.m., Sunday 11 a.m.–6 p.m.

Lazlo's Brewery & Grill

Food: American

710 P St.
Haymarket

(402) 434-5636

*www.telesis-inc.com/lazlo/
index.html*

Cool Features: They brew
their own ale, which parents
like, Brewer's Club, fun
events

Price: $12 and under
per person

Hours: Sunday–Thursday
11 a.m.–10 p.m., Friday–
Saturday 11 a.m.–11 p.m.

Misty's Steakhouse
and Brewery

Food: Steak

200 N. 11th St.

(402) 476-7766

www.mistyslincoln.com

Cool Features: They brew
their own beer, make their
own seasonings, they hold
banquets, catering

Price: $30 and under
per person

Hours: Monday–Thursday
11 a.m.–10 p.m., Friday–
Saturday 11 a.m.–11 p.m.,
Sunday 4 p.m.–11 p.m.

Old Chicago

Food: American, pizza

826 P St.
Haymarket

(402) 477-2277

Cool Features: There's a bar
with pool tables and a party
room upstairs, gorge yourself
on giant helpings of food

Price: $10 and under
per person

Hours: Sunday–Monday
11 a.m.–12 a.m.

Papa John's Pizza

Food: Pizza delivery

1601 Q St.

(402) 476-6262

www.papajohns.com

Cool Features: Cheap pizza
that's delivered to your door

Price: $7 and under
per person

Hours: Daily 11 a.m.–11 p.m.

Perkin's Restaurant

Food: American

2900 N.W. 12th St.

(402) 474-6162

www.perkinsrestaurants.com

Cool Features: Yummy
homemade desserts

Price: $10 and under
per person

Hours: 24 hours daily

Taste of China

Food: Chinese

1349 Q St.

(402) 475-3456

Cool Features: Take-out
and delivery

Price: $8 and under
per person

Hours: Daily
11 a.m.–9:30 p.m.

Valentino's To-Go

Food: Fast-food Italian

232 N. 13th St.

(402) 475-1501

Cool Features: Take-out,
buffet that will leave you full
for a week

Price: $10 and under
per person

Hours: Sunday–Thursday
11 a.m.–10 p.m., Friday–
Saturday 11 a.m.–11 p.m.

YiaYia's Pizza

Food: Pizza

1423 O St.

(402) 477-9166

Cool Features: Serves thin-
crust pizza and drinks in a
dimly lit room with loud music
and pool tables

Price: $5 and under
per person

Hours: Daily 11 a.m.–12 a.m.

Did You Know?

There are **more than 100 restaurants** within walking
distance of the UNL campus. It's a blessing but also
a curse because the wide selection baffles many
indecisive students who will sometimes spend a half
hour debating where to eat.

Student Favorites:

Amigos Mexican Restaurant
Bison Witches Bar & Deli
Buffalo Wild Wings
Chipotle
Doozy's
Ivanna Cone
Jimmy John's
Gourmet Sandwiches
Juice Stop
Lazlo's Brewery & Grill
Papa John's Pizza
Valentino's To-Go

Late-Night Dining:

Amigos Mexican Restaurant

24-Hour Eating:

Perkin's Restaurant

Closest
Grocery Stores:

Hy-Vee
2343 N. 48th St.
(402) 467-5505

Super Saver
2662 Cornhusker Highway
(402) 466-7100

Wal-Mart Super Center
4700 N. 27th St.
(402) 438-4377

Best Pizza:

YiaYia's Pizza

Best Chinese:

Taste of China

Best Breakfast:

Bruegger's Bagels

Best Wings:

Buffalo Wild Wings

Best Healthy:

Juice Stop

Best Place to Take
Your Parents:

Lazlo's Brewery & Grill

Students Speak Out On...
Off-Campus Dining

"There are quite a few good ones. I like Misty's Steakhouse, Firework's, and Lazlo's. Also, fast food is everywhere."

Q "They have the same restaurants that most larger cities have. **Lazlo's stands out above the rest**."

Q "There is an area near campus called the Haymarket, an **old part of the downtown that has been made over** and is now a very good place to find some yummy food. Some good restaurants in and around this area are Lazlo's, FireWork's, a couple of Mexican places, and Old Chicago. Finding a good restaurant near campus is not hard."

Q "I **can't afford to eat out much**, but I really like Doozy's. It's a sandwich shop in downtown Lincoln. It's pretty good. My other favorite place is Buzzard Billy's. It's authentic Cajun and Creole cuisine, and located in the Haymarket. My parents' favorite is Lazlo's, and I'd have to agree that it is pretty good as well."

Q "Since Lincoln is a college town, there are many restaurants within walking distance of campus. **There are also a lot of places that deliver**—a favorite is Jimmy John's that delivers subs until 2 a.m. Amigos is also open late."

Q "Off campus, **there are some great pasta, pizza, and sub places that deliver**. The restaurants in Lincoln are definitely good."

Q "UNL is right downtown, so **if you don't have a car you can walk to all the bars, restaurants, and movie theatres**. Jimmy John's will occupy a special place in your heart. They are great for when you get the drunken munchies because they deliver late."

Q "There are **lots of restaurants near campus**. There are the obvious fast-food places, some of which are open as late as 4 a.m. Then there are the 'real' restaurants in the Haymarket, which is in walking distance. Omaha is an hour away and there are tons of places there, too!"

The College Prowler Take On...
Off-Campus Dining

UNL students are pleased with Lincoln restaurants. Of course there are the big chains, but what students really like are the strictly local places that are scattered throughout downtown and the Haymarket. As for late-night and delivery (two key factors in a college student's diet), there are sandwich shops, Mexican, Chinese, and pizza places that stay open until the wee hours of the morning.

There are some really great restaurants in town, and none of them will cost you an arm and a leg. There are also plenty of culinary options for first dates, parent's weekend, and 21st birthday bashes. All-in-all, the dining scene in Lincoln will satisfy even the pickiest eater's tastebuds.

B+

The College Prowler® Grade on

Off-Campus Dining: B+

A high Off-Campus Dining grade implies that off-campus restaurants are affordable, accessible, and worth visiting. Other factors include the variety of cuisine and the availability of alternative options (vegetarian, vegan, Kosher, etc.).

Campus Housing

The Lowdown On...
Campus Housing

Room Types:
Singles, doubles, triples, suites (single rooms with shared living room, kitchen, bathroom, and balcony), apartments

Best Dorms:
Abel Hall
Selleck Quad

Worst Dorms:
Sandoz Hall

Undergrads Living on Campus:
24%

Number of Dorms:
14

Universtiy-Owned Apartments:
2

→

Dormitories:

Abel Hall
Floors: 13
Total Occupancy: 1004
Bathrooms: Shared by floor
Coed: Yes
Residents: Upperclassmen
Room Types: Double, super double
Special Features: Refrigerator, loftable bed, recreation area, study area, computer lab, cable, gameroom, laundry, air conditioning, elevator, biggest dorm, first eight floors house Residential Learning Community to help residents adjust and develop study skills

Burr Hall
Floors: 3
Total Occupancy: 222
Bathrooms: Shared by floor
Coed: Yes
Residents: Freshmen, sophomore, junior, senior
Room Types: Double
Special Features: Recreation area, study area, computer lab, cable, gameroom, laundry, air conditioning, shuttle to city campus, Microfridge, close-knit community, home to Achievement, Commitment, and Excellence

Cather Hall
Floors: 13
Total Occupancy: 228
Bathrooms: Shared by floor
Coed: Yes
Residents: Mostly upperclassmen
Room Types: Single, double
Special Features: Study area, computer lab, cable, gameroom, laundry, air conditioning, Microfridge, elevator, recreation area, home of International Theme Housing, which provides activities reflecting an international interest

Fedde Hall
Floors: 3
Total Occupancy: 39
Bathrooms: Shared by floor
Coed: Yes
Residents: Upperclassmen and graduate students
Room Types: Single
Special Features: Microfridge, recreation area, study area, computer lab, cable, gameroom, laundry, air conditioning, small and quiet community, shuttle to city campus

Harper Hall

Floors: 10

Total Occupancy: 450

Bathrooms: Shared by floor

Coed: Yes

Residents: Upperclassmen and graduate students

Room Types: Double, super double

Special Features: Study area, computer lab, cable, gameroom, laundry, air conditioning, recreation area, elevator, staff helps residents adjust and learn life skills

Husker Hall

Floors: 3

Total Occupancy: 41

Bathrooms: Shared by floor

Coed: Yes

Residents: Graduate and non-traditonal

Room Types: Single

Special Features: Prepare meals in the hall kitchen, study area, computer lab, cable, gameroom, laundry, air conditioning, Microfridge in room, shuttle to city and east campus

Husker Courtyard

Floors: 5

Total Occupancy: 478

Bathrooms: In apartment

Coed: Yes

Residents: Upperclassmen, graduate, non-traditional freshmen

Room Types: Two- and four-bedroom apartments

Special Features: Living area, full kitchen, patio, storage room, cable hookup, two free meals a week, basic bathroom cleaning every other week

Husker Village

Floors: 5

Total Occupancy: 528

Bathrooms: In apartment

Coed: Yes

Residents: Upperclassmen

Room Types: Two- and four-bedroom apartments

Special Features: Living area, full kitchen, storage room, cable hookup, convenience store with lounge and fireplace, two free meals a week, basic bathroom cleaning every other week

Kauffman Center

Floors: 3

Total Occupancy: 200

Bathrooms: Private

Coed: Yes

Residents: Freshmen, sophomores, juniors, seniors

Room Types: Suite-style

Special Features: Study area, TV lounge, game room, laundry, home to J.D. Edwards Honors Program

Love Memorial Coop

Floors: 3

Total Occupancy: 45

Bathrooms: Shared by floor

Coed: No, just females

Residents: Upperclassmen

Room Types: Double

Special Features: Self-governed, supportive academic and social environment, no board plan, home-cooked meals, close parking, shuttle to city campus, all residents share house duties

Neihardt Hall

Floors: 3

Total Occupancy: 462

Bathrooms: Shared by floor

Coed: Yes

Residents: Freshmen, sophomores, juniors, seniors

(Neihardt Hall, continued)

Room Types: Double

Special Features: Loft-beds, sinks in rooms, study area, computer lab, cable, gameroom, laundry, air conditioning, home of Honors Program

Pound Hall

Floors: 13

Total Occupancy: 228

Bathrooms: Shared by floor

Coed: Yes

Residents: Mostly upperclassmen

Room Types: Single

Special Features: Study area, computer lab, cable, gameroom, laundry, air conditioning, recreation area, house Honors Program

Sandoz Hall

Floors: 9

Total Occupancy: 465

Bathrooms: Shared by floor

Coed: Yes

Residents: Mostly freshmen, also upperclassmen

Room Types: Double, triple

Special Features: Recreation and study area, computer lab, cable, gameroom, laundry, air conditioning, MicroFridge, home to many sororities pledges

Schramm Hall

Floors: 10

Total Occupancy: 450

Bathrooms: Shared by floor

Coed: Yes

Residents: All classes

Room Types: Double, super double

Special Features: Recreation area, study area, computer lab, cable, gameroom, laundry, air conditioning, events for residents with an emphasis on acclimation to campus and study skills

Smith Hall

Floors: 10

Total Occupancy: 450

Bathrooms: Shared by floor

Coed: Yes

Residents: Freshmen, sophomores

Room Types: Double, super double

Special Features: Recreation area, study area, computer lab, cable, gameroom, laundry, air conditioning, staff programming focuses on adjusting to campus, life skills, study habits

Selleck Quad

Floors: 3

Total Occupancy: 612

Bathrooms: Shared by floor

Coed: Yes

Residents: Graduates, non-traditional, undergraduates

Room Types: Double

Special Features: Central location, diverse population, dining service, study area, computer lab, cable, gameroom, laundry, air conditioning, facilities for physically challenged, International Theme Housing and Music Residential Learning Community with practice and music library

Housing Offered:

Singles: 16%

Doubles: 70%

Triples/Suites: 2%

Apartments: 12%

Available for Rent

Bed lofts, bed sheets, Microfridge, refrigerator

Bed Type

Twin extra-long

What You Get

Bed, desk, chair, closet, bookshelf, dresser, window coverings, cable, local phone line, Ethernet connection, air conditioning

Cleaning Service?

A professional cleaning service takes pride in cleaning the public areas on campus, but your room is your business.

Also Available

You can pay a little extra for linen service, which saves you the hassle of washing your sheets.

Did You Know?

Tommy Lee's **Neidhardt Hall dorm room was actually an apartment** complex right in downtown Lincoln.

Students Speak Out On...
Campus Housing

"The dorms were an experience, I guess. I lived in Abel, which is historically the party hall. Unless you're into academics hardcore, avoid Neihardt and Kauffman. Sandoz— stay away from it, as well."

Q "The dorms all have a reputation. Harper, Schramm, and Smith seem to be the best. It is a **large complex full of people, making it easy to find people** in your class or friends. I would live there in comparison to Abel because you don't have to cross more than two streets to get to campus. Also, I think parking is easier at HSS. Abel is the party dorm that is coed by not only floor, but by building. Selleck is known as the international dorm, full of upperclassmen and exchange students. It is the closest to campus, right by the union. Fun place, but if you live there you might feel much younger than the others. Pound and Cather also have a majority of upperclassmen."

Q "I lived in Abel, a coed dorm, and it was definitely more fun. It's all about what you want—**a place to meet and greet and have fun, or a place to relax and study**. I think I would've preferred the quiet dorm now because I could go somewhere to have fun. I had nowhere to retreat in Abel when I needed some peace."

Q "Live in either Abel or Sandoz. I wish I would have lived in Sandoz—it's quieter. It is connected to Abel, which is coed by wings, boys at one end of the hall and girls at the other. Plus **Abel and Sandoz are closer to downtown**, the gas station is right there, and closer to a lot of the campus buildings."

Q "Dorms are the best. I would suggest that if you do not rush, that you live in Selleck. That is where I live and I love it. It is the best dorm because it is the center of campus. Dorms to avoid: **Abel/Sandoz is the party-dorm—most dropouts come out of there**. And Harper Schramm Smith complex—it is pretty far from campus. Stick with Selleck. The food is prepared the best on campus there."

Q "Harper, Schramm, and Smith are coed by floor and are pretty cool. **Neihardt is the honors dorm**. You have to be in the honors program to live there. It's coed by floor, but some floors suck and others are really cool (and you don't get to pick). If you are in the J.D. Edwards honors program you have to live in Kauffman, and it is very nice, but very studious. Overall, I would suggest Harper, Schramm, Smith, or Abel."

Q "The dorms are very fun. **I would recommend living in them your first year**. If you want to meet guys I would recommend living in Abel because there will be guys living on the same floor with you. Most American freshmen don't live in Selleck—that tends to be the international housing dorm."

Q "The dorms are good overall—**they're very safe and well organized**."

Q "**I never lived in one** and I'm very glad."

The College Prowler Take On...
Campus Housing

When it comes to picking favorites, UNL students care more about the convenience and reputation of a dorm than the quality of its rooms. Some students are willing to sacrifice shut-eye for partying (Abel), while others are willing to walk three extra blocks to class so they can actually study in their rooms (at Harper-Schramm-Smith). Students really enjoy living on campus, but many feel that it's important to choose a dorm with a personality that matches their own.

Perhaps more importantly, there are many strong friendships that are bound while living on campus. At UNL, all freshmen are required to live on campus during their first years, which means the dorms have a wide variety of residents. Even if you aren't BFF (best friends forever) with your roommate, you're bound to meet someone you like on your floor—there are like 60 to 100 other undergrads. It has been proven that students are truly better off living like sardines their freshman years than living the suite life, just for the bonding experience. The friendships you will forge in the dorms will make your college years that much more meaningful and fun.

The College Prowler® Grade on
Campus Housing: B-

A high Campus Housing grade indicates that dorms are clean, well-maintained, and spacious. Other determining factors include variety of dorms, proximity to classes, and social atmosphere.

Off-Campus Housing

The Lowdown On...
Off-Campus Housing

Undergrads in Off-Campus Housing:
76%

Average Rent For:
Studio/Apartment: $350
1BR Apartment: $350
2BR Apartment: $550

Popular Areas:
17th to 33rd Streets
Claremont Apartments
Holdrege to Vine Streets
Stadium View Apartments

For Assistance Contact:
Commuter Student Services
http://asun.unl.edu/page.php?page_id=3
(402) 472-2581

Best Time to Look for a Place

March is a good time to start scoping out your options. Keep in mind that most renters don't know their availability until a month in advance, however. Lincoln leases tend to run August to August. Good luck trying to find a six-month lease.

Students Speak Out On...
Off-Campus Housing

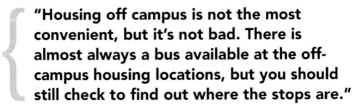

"Housing off campus is not the most convenient, but it's not bad. There is almost always a bus available at the off-campus housing locations, but you should still check to find out where the stops are."

Q "It is way cheaper than CU. However, getting on and off campus isn't the easiest. There is this ridiculous **rule that not more than three unrelated people can live together**. They are building a lot of parking garages, making parking for commuters easier."

Q "There are a few apartment complexes and houses to rent that are within a walk to campus, but not many. **Most are not in the best shape either**."

Q "I live off campus and love it. The dorms were fun while I lived there, but you have to grow up and move on sometime. I live right by East Campus. **There are shuttles that run to and from the two campuses** every 10 minutes. It's not bad at all. If you live somewhere else, you'd have to drive in."

Q "Housing is very convenient. I am going to live off of campus next semester. **Rent is typically cheap**."

Q "Since the town mostly caters to college students, there are **many apartments and duplexes around**. There are also separate parking passes sold to students who live off campus."

Q "Housing off campus is **really close and rather affordable**. I have tons of friends off campus. Sometimes the houses are so close to campus, it doesn't feel like it's any different than living on campus."

Q "**I don't think it's too hard to find off-campus housing**. There are apartment guides all over, especially in the newspaper and on the bulletin boards that many people advertise."

Q "I personally live off campus right now and all last year and it's pretty convenient. There is an apartment complex right by campus and it's all college kids. It's fun going there because **there is always something going on**."

Q "**Anything from a 20-minute walk to a 20-minute drive**. It depends on what you want to do."

Q "**Most off-campus housing does require that you drive** or bike to class in the mornings, but no place takes longer than about 10 minutes to get to campus from."

Q "Off-campus housing is **convenient and affordable**. Look, look, look. Remember: find someone you will be able to handle living with."

Q "Off-campus housing is a great option. There are apartments and houses for cheap rates and **they range in quality and conveniance**."

The College Prowler Take On...
Off-Campus Housing

As they grow older, students embark on a whole new world: off-campus living. UNL students have fond memories of the dorms, but there comes a time when students feel they need their own place. Lucky for them, there are quite a few places in and around Lincoln for a kid to call home. The commute is the largest concern among off-campus students and they recommend never straying too far from the nest. Also, many students prefer to live in the college communities surrounding campus.

With three out of four UNL students living off campus, off-campus living is highly sought after. You probably won't live in a mansion or cook anything more advanced than pasta or cereal, but it's college after all.

B+

The College Prowler® Grade on

Off-Campus Housing: B+

A high grade in Off-Campus Housing indicates that apartments are of high quality, close to campus, affordable, and easy to secure.

Diversity

The Lowdown On...
Diversity

Native American:
1%

African American:
2%

Asian American:
2%

Hispanic:
2%

White:
90%

International:
3%

Out-of-State:
20%

Political Activity

Campus is split fairly evenly between Republicans and Democrats. There are a handful of students who are visible on campus as the political type, but sadly, the political activism of our parents' generation has dwindled from flames to mere flickers.

Gay Pride

UNL has its fair share of homophobes, which isn't too surprising considering Nebraska was one of the first states to ban gay marriage in its constitution. But for every foe there's a friend, and fortunately, the UNL administration is a great friend to the gay student body.

Most Popular Religions

Students at UNL represent many different religions, but Lutherans and Catholics dominate the spiritual scene.

Economic Status

The majority of UNL students drive a '97 Honda, wear Gap clothing and pay $15 for a haircut. Nebraska is not a rich state and the UNL student body accurately depicts the state's average income level. As a result, the students here are more down-to-earth. People aren't judged by where they bought their shoes or whether or not their daddy paid for the new campus building.

Minority Clubs

African Peoples Union, Chinese language & Cultural Exchange, Mexican American Student Association, Minorities in Agricultural Natural Resources, Multicultural Legal Society, Vietnamese Student Assocation, Spectrum

Students Speak Out On...
Diversity

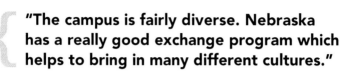

"The campus is fairly diverse. Nebraska has a really good exchange program which helps to bring in many different cultures."

Q "The campus is predominately white, but you see fliers for minority groups everywhere. It's **not too hard to find a group of people with whom you're comfortable**."

Q "It's very diverse. There are **a lot of Asians and Middle Eastern people**."

Q "You will meet all kinds of people in Nebraska. There are also **many different cultural events that you can go to**, and a culture center."

Q "I hate to say it, but the **majority of UNL students are white**."

Q "Considering the fact that it is Nebraska, it's pretty diverse. However, it's **primarily white Americans at UNL**."

Q "**We have lots of Asians**, but it is predominantly white."

Q "**The campus is very, very diverse**, and some dormitories are more diverse than others. If you are looking to stay in a diverse dorm, I recommend Selleck Hall."

Q "UNL has a low minority level, but it seems like that nationwide. The University is trying hard though. UNL has **many events to diversify their campus**, though."

Q "It's not very diverse. I feel this is the biggest flaw. The campus is more than 90 percent white. There is little encouragement of diversity either. **There's also an anti-gay sentiment on the campus.**"

Q "Don't come here if you want diversity. You will not find it, even **if you venture off campus, it gets worse** and worse."

Q "We are **not known for being that much of a diverse campus**; it's mostly white over here, that's about it."

Q "Well, **we have all kinds of European ancestry**! There's very little diversity from a non-diverse state."

The College Prowler Take On...
Diversity

It's not that students don't want diversity at UNL, there's just not a whole lot of it to be had in the great state of Nebraska. Many of the minority students at UNL are honors students, student leaders, and they are greeted with the same warm smile that anyone else could expect from a Nebraskan.

Of course there's progress to be made at UNL when it comes to diversity, and some may argue that there is nowhere to go but up. Racial stereotypes and slurs certainly don't run rampant, but they're not unheard of either. In 1892, George Flippin put on his Nebraska football helmet to become one of only five African-American student-athletes in the nation. It's this kind of forward thinking that UNL strives for—even in a state that can be a bit backwards, and for this the school earns some points (but not enough for a decent grade).

The College Prowler® Grade on

Diversity: D-

A high grade in Diversity indicates that ethnic minorities and international students have a notable presence on campus and that students of different economic backgrounds, religious beliefs, and sexual preferences are well-represented.

Guys & Girls

The Lowdown On...
Guys & Girls

Men Undergrads:
53%

Women Undergrads:
47%

Birth Control Available?
Yes, at the University Health Center

Most Prevalent STDs on Campus
Chlamydia and genital warts

Percentage of Students with an STD
About 5% of UNL students report an STD during their college careers

Social Scene

Most students are outgoing and have no trouble going out for a night on the town. UNL breeds social butterflies, not bookworms, and it shows in the masses of college kids who flutter off to the bars, restaurants, and coffee shops at night.

Hookups or Relationships?

Plenty of girls leave UNL with an MRS degree, but if you want a casual fling, you won't be alone. There are many students looking for a good time and they're pretty easy to spot. But the main sentiment on campus is, "if it happens, it happens."

Best Place to Meet Guys/Girls

Classes and parties are the most common places to meet. I'm sure that more than a few marriages began in an astronomy class at UNL. On a less romantic note, I'm also sure that even more marriages were spawned at loud booze-fests inside some old decrepit house.

Dress Code

Students attend class in very casual clothes—there will be days when almost every student in class is wearing a sweatshirt and a baseball hat to cover their unwashed hair. At night, however, students transform themselves into MTV poster-children and the clothing competition can be fierce.

Did You Know?

Top Three Places to Find Hotties:

1. O Street on the weekend
2. Frat parties
3. The Student Union

Top Places to Hook Up:

1. Love Library stacks
2. Fraternity houses (not sororities)
3. Dorm room (while your roommate's in class)
4. House parties
5. Broyhill Fountain

Students Speak Out On...
Guys & Girls

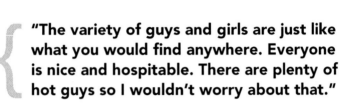

{ **"The variety of guys and girls are just like what you would find anywhere. Everyone is nice and hospitable. There are plenty of hot guys so I wouldn't worry about that."**

Q "Guys—**very hot**."

Q "Guys and girls are **a little more casual** and dressed down, but that doesn't take away from their faces. They are both good looking."

Q "The guys are average. It seems to be like everywhere else I've been. There are definitely some hotties, and then **there are those gross, nasty losers** whom you'd like to get away from ASAP!"

Q "Most of the **girls sure are hot**!"

Q "You have **really good and really bad**."

Q "Here's where I'm going to be blunt—you may not see uglier people anywhere but here. A lot of people are stuck in some time warp. Others just appear not to care. Don't get me wrong, there is occasionally a cute guy here and there, but **they're few and far between**."

Q "There are a lot of good-looking boys at Nebraska. All different kinds too. Plenty of **preppy fraternity boys**, if that's what you like, and plenty of hot non-fraternity boys, too."

Q "**The girls are really nice and friendly**. You will make lots of friends in your classes and the dorms."

Q "Compared to high school, there are more boys and girls than you'll know what to do with. It depends on your taste, but out of 11,000 men on campus **I'm sure you can find one that meets your needs**."

Q "Guys and girls are the same as you will find on any big college campus. There are the **hot ones, the cute ones, the generic ones, the not-so-hot ones**."

Q "Because the Greek system is somewhat big, guys and girls tend to be competitive, so **people tend to dress well when they go out**."

Q "There are a lot of hot guys here, and there are lots of pretty girls and I'm sure **you won't have trouble finding what you are looking for**."

Q "I'd have to say, Nebraskans are by far **some of the nicest people in this country**."

Q "**It's like heaven here**. Everyone is gorgeous."

Q "Can't say nothing about the guys really, and the girls are all right, but **there are some hot ones now and then**."

Q "Everyone here is very friendly, hot and approachable. You are **guaranteed to get laid over here**, trust me!"

Q "There are **beautiful people of all types**—not just jocks. Seek, and you will find."

The College Prowler Take On...
Guys & Girls

Either UNL students have really low standards, or the guys and girls really are as good-looking as the students claim. Students commonly mention members of the Greek system as the Adonis's and Aphrodite's of UNL, but there's also a feeling among students that there are plenty of great and interesting mortals out there to spend eternity with.

UNL is not quite as sex-crazed as many other large public universities, but it's not entirely celibate either. Campus legend says that if a girl goes through her four years at UNL without hooking up, then one of the school's beloved columns will topple. As of today, they're all standing.

The College Prowler® Grade on

Guys: B

A high grade for Guys indicates that the male population on campus is attractive, smart, friendly, and engaging, and that the school has a decent ratio of guys to girls.

The College Prowler® Grade on

Girls: B-

A high grade for Girls not only implies that the women on campus are attractive, smart, friendly, and engaging, but also that there is a fair ratio of girls to guys.

Athletics

The Lowdown On...
Athletics

Athletic Division:
NCAA Division I

Conference:
Big 12

Mascot:
Herbie Husker

School Colors:
Scarlet and Cream

Males Playing Varsity Sports:
387 (5%)

Females Playing Varsity Sports:
218 (3%)

➡

Men's Varsity Sports:

Baseball
Basketball
Cross Country
Football
Golf
Gymnastics
Tennis
Track and Field
Wrestling

Women's Varsity Sports:

Basketball
Bowling
Cross Country
Golf
Gymnastics
Rifle
Soccer
Softball
Swimming and Diving
Tennis
Track and Field
Volleyball

Club Sports:

Baseball
Climbing
Crew (Rowing)
Cycling
Handball
Hockey (Ice)

(Club Sports, continued)

Hockey (Roller)
Judo
Lacrosse
Paintball
Racquetball
Rifle
Rugby
Runners
Ski/Snowboard
Soccer
Sport Officials
Swimming
Synchronized Swimming
Table Tennis
Tae Kwon Do
Ultimate Frisbee
Water Polo

Intramurals:

Air Hockey
Air Rifle
Archery
Badminton
Basketball
Bench Press
Bowling
Broomball
Chess
Climbing Wall
Cross Country
Dodgeball
Flag Football
Floor Hockey

(Intramurals, continued)

Foosball	Pool
Golf	Punt, Pass, and Kick
Horseshoe	Quickball
Indoor Soccer	Racquetball
Indoor Track	Rifle Shoot
Inner Tube Water Basketball	Softball
Kickball	Table Tennis
Laser Quest	Tennis
Miniature Golf	Tug-of-War
Obstacle Course	Ultimate
Outdoor Track	Volleyball
	Wrestling

Most Popular Sports

Baseball, football, men's basketball, volleyball

Athletic Fields

Bob Devaney Sports Center

This five-acre sports complex contains a 13,500-seat basketball arena an 5,000-seat indoor track with seating, a 10-lane swimming pool and diving well, and gymnastics and wrestling facilities.

Haymarket Park

This is the 750-seat softball and baseball stadium complete with concessions, press box, and skybox suites, heated dugouts, a training room, a weight room, and a player's lounge.

Memorial Stadium

The place where tens of thousands have come to watch Husker football since 1923. This 80,000-seat complex also includes the Championship Indoor Center, a 120-yard field with an identical FieldTurf surface to the gameday surface.

Getting Tickets

Students get half-price tickets to football, volleyball, and basketball games. All other sporting events are free for UNL students. You have to plan far in advance to attend football and volleyball games, though.

Overlooked Teams

Gymnastics meets are great, and the Track & Field team is one of the best in the country. Both of these sporting events are free for students, which is a big perk considering what it costs to attend a football game.

Best Place to Take a Walk

The artsy side of City Campus is nice because there are trickling fountains and cool sculptures everywhere. All of East Campus is very pretty to walk through—make sure to stop by the gazebo.

Gyms/Facilities

The City Campus Rec Center is spectacular and has all the regular gym equipment plus classes, trainers, a climbing wall, racquetball courts, an indoor track, five basketball/volleyball/ badminton courts, an indoor football/soccer field, a lap pool, and massage therapists. The East Campus Rec Center is pretty crummy, however, and is one of the only buildings on campus without air conditioning.

Did You Know?

Tommy Lee tried out and made the Husker band as part of the drumline. After the game, he headed down to O Street and shared a few drinks with his fellow band members.

Students Speak Out On...
Athletics

"Husker sports are huge. Football is the main attraction, although women's volleyball and gymnastics, and men's baseball are usually solid. IM sports have a lot to offer."

Q "Lots of sports! **Everyone plays sports** up here!"

Q "Varsity sports on campus are huge. The University of Nebraska **prides itself on many of its athletics**. The football, volleyball, baseball, and softball teams are among the best in the nation. Intramural sports on campus are decent. I never really had time to participate in them, but I see many people playing them all the time."

Q "Sports are huge! They are **all about their football—believe me**. I don't blame them since they don't have much in Nebraska. They focus on their college team since they don't have any professional teams. Other sports are big too, as well as IM."

Q "Well, football *is* Nebraska. **People bleed Husker Red** here—it's pathetic frankly. They even sell our parking spaces here for the home games and make the students park elsewhere. Basketball isn't really supported here, but the women's volleyball team is. They just built a new baseball/softball stadium as well."

Q "Very good. **IM sports are really big on campus** especially with Greeks."

Q "Well, if you know anything about Nebraska, you know we love football. Even if you are not that big of a football fan when you get here, that will change. The **campus practically shuts down on Football Saturdays**. Intramurals are also very big on campus. Most dorm floors will get together an intramural team, as well as the Greek houses. There are many different sports to choose from: flag football, volleyball, basketball, soccer, or softball. You can also choose to do it all-girls or coed. If you are into working out, we have the best rec center in the nation—that is an actual statistic! It's free for students to use the courts, rent balls, use the weight room and treadmills, and there is also a track. Another perk is that you can take aerobics classes and step classes, or you can even get a great massage."

Q "Sports at UNL are insane. **You have never seen such diehard fans**, especially when it comes to football and volleyball. Football games are nuts. There is tailgating all day and the games are so intense. You will have no idea till you go to one. IM sports are tons of fun to play in and watch. Basically, any sport you can think of—volleyball, basketball, football, even things like synchronized swimming and miniature golf."

Q "Varsity sports are huge. **This campus lives for them**. Football is king here, as you should know. (If you don't, act like you do!) Also, volleyball is great (lots of championships), baseball is still doing well this season, softball just lost out of the College World Series, and basketball is pretty bad but getting much, much better. Plus the Big 12 has lots of good teams, so the competition is fierce (especially in football since they all hate us—it's great!). IM is so fun, too. There is almost anything you can think of, and it's easy to sign up or get one started."

Q "Sports are huge at Nebraska. As you probably know **our football team, year in and year out, is vying for the National Championship**. You honestly haven't lived until you go to a home game at night. Football isn't the only thing going good for Nebraska sports-wise. Our softball team recently won the Women's College World Series, and our baseball team recently made it to the College World Series for the third time in a decade. Our volleyball team usually makes it to the National Championship tournament and has won it a bunch of times. Track and Field just won the Big 12 title and wrestling is good, too. Intramurals are a ton of fun. We have everything from broomball to soccer."

Q "Sports are b-i-g. But **you can avoid them**—trust me."

The College Prowler Take On...
Athletics

Students are well aware that, to the rest of the world, Nebraska is synonymous with Husker football. Athletics are a typical UNL student's pride and joy. Even if they're not on a sports scholarship, many UNL students are active in their own sport, whether through one of the many popular intramural sports offered, or through one of the best recreational centers in the nation.

In Nebraska, countless songs have been composed about the "Sea of Red" at Husker games at Memorial Stadium. There are only a few spectacles (the Grand Canyon, Niagara Falls, and the Running of the Bulls are some examples) that are more breathtaking than 100,000 screaming Nebraskans all in scarlet. The school spirit is addictive and even the most apathetic sports fans can't help but jump out of their seats and yell, "Go Big Red!"

The College Prowler® Grade on

Athletics: A

A high grade in Athletics indicates that students have school spirit, that sports programs are respected, that games are well-attended, and that intramurals are a prominent part of student life.

Nightlife

The Lowdown On...
Nightlife

Club and Bar Prowler:
Popular Nightlife Spots!

Club Crawler:
Bricktop

1427 O St.

(402) 476-4468

www.thebricktop.net

If you like to dance, this is your spot—theme nights, parties, drink specials, happy hour, and fun.

Knickerbockers

901 O St.

(402) 476-6865

www.knickerbockers.net

Knickerbockers is the place to go to hear live and local bands everyday of the week.

Q

226 S. 9th St.

(402) 475-2269

Q is Lincoln's one-and-only gay club. If you're in the

➔

(Q, continued)

mood to dance to pop or techno music, watch a drag show, play games, or hang out with a fun assortment of gay men, lesbians, straight girls and some heterosexual men, this is the place to go.

Sur Tango Bar & Café

1228 P St.

(402) 438-1222

www.surtangobar.com

This bar is an alternative entertaining atmosphere that offers gourmet coffees, international wines, and special drinks; listen to Spanish and Latin American music or take tango lessons.

Bar Prowler:

Brass Rail

1436 O St.

(402) 474-5741

The Rail is the best place to be when the night's coming to an end. The line may be a little long, but it's worth the wait. The Rail was once voted the Top Bar by *Playboy*.

Buffalo Wild Wings

1328 P St.

(402) 475-2999

www.buffalowildwings.com

Half-restaurant, half-bar; BW3's is very popular for large groups, especially groups with underagers.

Downtown

1430 O St.

(402) 435-7442

Filled with preppy people, socialize or shake your groove thing on the dance floor.

Cliff's Smoke Shop/Lounge

140 N. 12th St.

(402) 476-7997

Cliff's is not a hot-spot but its very intimate. It's been around for three decades, so it caters to an older crowd.

Duffy's Tavern

1412 O St.

(402) 474-3543

http://duffysrocks.dainto.org

The entertainment here includes comedy workshops, karaoke, live bands, and nightly drink specials.

Fat Nappys

5100 N. 48th St.

(402) 466-6644

www.fatnappys.com

Book your own party, watch a band, drink everything out of 16 oz. cups, or play in Lincoln's largest beer garden, which includes a stage and a volleyball court

Iguana's

1426 O St.

(402) 476-8850

Fun drinks and a fun atomosphere right in the middle of all of the fun on O Street.

Main St. Café

1325 O St.

(402) 435-1717

Main St. Café is a hot Greek hangout. Sometimes, it is not quite as highly-regarded as the Peach Pit (90210).

Mickey's Irish Pub

1409 O St.

(402) 438-3311

Mickey's added a cage. And throughout the night the DJ will yell over the mike, "No dudes in the cage!"

Old Chicago

826 P St.
Haymarket

(402) 477-2277

Upstairs can get pretty crowded on the weekends as UNL students drink beer play pool and eat really good pizza.

Red Fox Steak House and Lounge

1339 W. O St.

(402) 438-3300

At midnight girls will set down their drinks (or not) and dance on the bar.

Sandy's

1401 O St.

(402) 475-2418

Elk Creek Water (a mixture of every liquor on the rail) is about the only reason to go but what a reason it is.

Spigot Lounge

1624 O St.

(402) 435-4582

The Spigot is dingy and old, but it's also a classic so people keep going back.

Lazarri's

1434 O St.

(402) 475-5556

On a nice night, you can typically find about twenty students eating pizza and drinking beer on the patio in front of Lazarri's.

Woody's Pub

101 N. 14th St. #6

(402) 438-8383

If you're in the market for an athlete, go to Woody's.

YiaYia's Pizza, Beer & Wine

1423 O St.

(402) 477-9166

YiaYia's is more known for it's pizza than its bar, but that doesn't stop UNL students from going there on Friday and Saturday nights. And no, the name has nothing to do with the Ya Ya Sisterhood.

Zen's

122 N. 11th St. #2

(402) 475-2929

Zen's is the yuppie place where everybody really does know your name.

Other Places to Check Out:

Chatterbox

Marz Intergalactic Shrimp & Martini Bar

Starlite Lounge

Bars Close At:

1 a.m.

Student Favorites:

Anywhere on O Street

Favorite Drinking Games:

Bus Driver

Card Games

Flip Cup

Moose

Quarters

Primary Areas with Nightlife:

Downtown

O Street

Local Specialties:

Cliff's - Shark Water

Duffy's - Fishbowls

Iguana's - Iggy Juice

Mickey's - Red Leprechaun

Sandy's - Elk Creek Water

What to Do if You're Not 21

The Coffee House

1324 P St., (402) 477-6611

www.borntobewired.com/about.html

This place is "born to be wired;" listen to blues, jazz, or reggae, and live entertainment on the weekends.

The Loft at the Mill

800 P St., Haymarket, (402) 475-5522

www.loftatthemill.org

This is a unique multi-disciplinary black-box stage that provides an arena for smart, edgy programming and a home for emerging artists and groups to grow and develop.

O Street—the actual street

Even if you aren't 21, go to O Street and listen to a starving artist play guitar. And you can always count on the vendor to give you the best $4 hotdog of your life.

Useful Resources for Nightlife

Ground Zero in Lincoln's Friday paper

Flyers on bulletin boards

www.lincolnbeat.com

Cheapest Place to Get a Drink

On thirsty Thursday's, Iguana's has 50-cent draws, but Mickey's draws are only 25 cents. At Spigot, if you buy your first beer in their glass you can keep the glass.

Organization Parties

The University Program Council (UPC) plans most events like talent shows, lectures, movies on the green, stand-up comedy, and concerts.

Frats

See the Greek section!

Students Speak Out On...
Nightlife

"The bars are okay when you first turn 21, but they get old fast. One of my favorites is Mickey's. If you're into the Greek scene, Iguana's or Woody's are popular."

Q "We have O Street which is basically a **row of bars that stretches out about four or five blocks**. There are also a lot of places to eat that are really nice. Another nice service that the University provides is 475-RIDE, which is a free cab service for anyone who has had a little too much fun."

Q "Well, the clubs off campus are not so good, especially if you are under 19. The age of majority in Nebraska is nineteen, which means that **you can't go into a club unless you are nineteen-plus**. The bars are very close to campus which is good because it means you don't have to drink and drive. There are a wide variety of very popular bars to choose from."

Q "The **bars and clubs seem to be where all the action is**. UNL keeps its partying in the bars/clubs."

Q "Well bars close here at 1 a.m. There are a few fun spots in Lincoln, but **there's more to do in Omaha** (one hour away)."

Q "I'm not much into that meat market stuff. When I go out, it's just to **relax and hang out with friends**. A place within walking distance of campus is BW3's. You have to be 18, and it's more like one of those places where you go to check people out."

Q "We have many bars downtown. **Most of them are close to one another** and within walking distance of campus. While I am not old enough to attend, I do know many people who do go and have a lot of fun."

Q "The bars are **perfect**."

Q "There are many bars and clubs to go to. Again, since Lincoln is a college town, **the main strip of bars and clubs is in walking distance of campus**."

Q "I am not twenty-one yet, but we have awesome bars in Lincoln. O Street, the main street through Lincoln, is packed from **Thursday through Saturday night full of college students**—extremely busy!"

Q "O Street is the main street in town, and is walking distance from campus. That is where all the bars and clubs that attract college kids are located and they are awesome. It is really a good time. You have to be 21 to get into any bar that does not serve food. In other words, there is only one bar downtown that minors can get into, and after 9 p.m. you have to be 21. **They are really strict on carding down here, too**."

Q "The bars here exist; I really don't know anything about them. Too much **fun to be had elsewhere**."

Q "O Street right by campus has a ton of bars which I hear are fun. I have only been there a few times for fraternity pinnings. **Good places to hear live music**."

The College Prowler Take On...
Nightlife

UNL students don't seem to have too much trouble having a good time on weekends, or any other night, for that matter. O Street is extremely popular for the 21-and-over crowd, but minors aren't totally out of luck. Certain clubs are 19-plus on select nights and 20-year-olds can still get a drink at a coffee shop (non-alcoholic). Students appreciate O Street's proximity to campus and the NU-On-Wheels (475-RIDE) Program for those nights that walking home three blocks is out of the question.

Dealing with the pervasive nightlife is a huge perk of living in a college town. There always seems to be enough to do to keep students out of (or sometimes into) trouble. Be warned—the Lincoln Police Department maintains a constant presence downtown. On busy nights, they line their cars in the middle of 'O' Street to keep watch over the crowd. As long as you're not puking on people or fighting, they'll usually just look the other way.

The College Prowler® Grade on

Nightlife: B+

A high grade in Nightlife indicates that there are many bars and clubs in the area that are easily accessible and affordable. Other determining factors include the number of options for the under-21 crowd and the prevalence of house parties.

Greek Life

The Lowdown On...
Greek Life

Number of Fraternities:	**Undergrad Men in Fraternities:**
27	13%
Number of Sororities:	**Undergrad Women in Sororities:**
14	18%

→

Fraternities on Campus:

Acacia

Alpha Gamma Nu

Alpha Gamma Rho

Alpha Gamma Sigma

Alpha Phi Alpha

Alpha Tau Omega

Beta Sigma Psi

Beta Theta Pi

Chi Phi

Delta Tau Delta

Delta Upsilon

Farmhouse

Iota Phi Theta

Kappa Alpha Psi

Lamda Chi Alpha

Omega Psi Phi

Phi Delta Theta

Phi Gamma Delta

Phi Kappa Psi

Pi Kappa Alpha

Sigma Alpha Epsilon

Sigma Chi

Sigma Lambda Beta

Sigma Nu

Sigma Phi Epsilon

Theta Xi

Triangle

Sororities on Campus:

Alpha Chi Omega

Alpha Delta Pi

Alpha Omicron Pi

Alpha Phi

Alpha Xi Delta

Chi Omega

Delta Delta Delta

Delta Gamma

Gamma Phi Beta

Kappa Alpha Theta

Kappa Delta

Kappa Kappa Gamma

Phi Mu

Pi Beta Phi

Other Greek Organizations:

Greek Council

Greek Peer Advisors

Interfraternity Council

Order of Omega

Panhellenic Council

Multicultural Colonies:

Alpha Kappa Alpha

Alpha Phi Alpha

Delta Sigma Theta

Iota Phi Theta

Kappa Alpha Psi

Lambda Phi Epsilon

Omega Psi Phi

Phi Beta Sigma

Sigma Gamma Rho

Sigma Lambda Beta

Sigma Lambda Gamma

Sigma Psi Zeta

Zeta Phi Beta

Did You Know?

Tommy Lee decided to join Alpha Gamma Nu, but after the **initiation duties of scrubbing toilets and doing dishes,** he decided to start his own fraternity. He established the House of Lee, a bright-red building with a Husker N on the roof.

UNL has **a $300,000 grant** to "re-evolve" the Greek system and save it from the *Animal House* stereotype of binge drinking and hazing.

Students Speak Out On...
Greek Life

"Greek life is prominent, but I wouldn't say it dominates. Nebraska is a dry campus, so the lack of alcohol takes the starch out of frat parties."

"The Greek Life at Nebraska is awesome. I am a little biased though because I am Greek. I wouldn't say it dominates the social scene, though. I knew plenty of people who weren't Greek and they never had a problem finding a party. **I would recommend going Greek especially if you are from out-of-state**."

"No, Greek life does not dominate the scene at all. If you end up in Sandoz dorm you will think it dominates the scene because those **girls are all about sororities**, or so I hear."

"**I couldn't imagine living in a house with so many girls**. As women, we're just naturally catty at times. I think that would be a nightmare. My brother joined and lived in a frat house for a few years. He really enjoyed it."

"I am currently checking out the fraternities and I will probably join one if I find some guys I like. As for dominating the scene, I didn't attend any Greek parties last semester, but I definitely would recommend the Greek system to anyone because of **its many benefits—both academic and social**."

Q "**Very good and strong**. I am VP of my house. The Greek systems get very involved—there are 16 fraternities and 14 sororities."

Q "Well, I think Greek life is great! UNL has a very strong Greek system. Since I am in a sorority, I know that being **Greek helps you meet a lot of new people** and there is always something to do. But that's not saying you have to be Greek to have fun on campus. I would encourage you to go through recruitment, though. Even if you decide not to pledge, you'll meet a lot of girls."

Q "I have no idea what people do at UNL who are not in the Greek system. Actually, one of my best friends was not in the Greek system and has decided to rush next year because **the party scene is way better**."

Q "I would seriously consider it. Even if it is not your thing, I would say you don't know until you try. A lot of **stereotypes are really wrong**. The Greek system's GPA is a lot higher than the University average; Greeks volunteer, and tend to be a lot more active on campus."

Q "I am in a sorority, but I have many non-Greek friends. **Greek life is a big part of our campus**, and right now it has been getting a bad rap because of an incident at a fraternity that happened a while back, but for the most part we try to come together and be of service. Sure, there are lots of parties and people talk about this sorority and that sorority and what's good and what's bad. Seriously, I have friends in almost every chapter, and that's okay. I also have non-Greek friends, too, and that's also okay. You can do whatever you want, and some people will say that you are stuck up if you are in a house, but they are the people who don't have a clue what Greek life is about. Some people will say you are a loser if you aren't in a house, but those are the stupid people who joined for all the wrong reasons. I tend to ignore them."

Q "It **does not dominate**, but I don't know anything about it."

Q "Greeks pretty much are everywhere on campus—it's **kind of annoying**."

Q "I am not a member of the Greek system, but I know it is very **fun for the girls and guys involved**. However, it does not dominate the campus and there is plenty to do without being involved in the Greek system."

Q "I wouldn't say it dominates the social scene, but **it plays a decent role**. I didn't rush myself, but that was just not for me. The sororities can be very catty."

The College Prowler Take On...
Greek Life

UNL students who choose to go Greek tend to like it, and students who decide to remain independent usually live productive lives too. Most people admit that the Greeks can sometimes dominate the social scene and they also admit that it's a fallible system. The general buzz around campus, however, is that there are a lot of great leadership, scholarship, and philanthropic opportunities for Greeks, and it's certainly an option worth considering.

There isn't much of a rivalry between the Greeks and the non-Greeks at UNL. As a matter of fact, many classrooms, organizations, and intramural teams are all a mix of Greeks and non-Greeks and everyone seems to get along.

B

The College Prowler® Grade on
Greek Life: B

A high grade in Greek Life indicates that sororities and fraternities are not only present, but also active on campus. Other determining factors include the variety of houses available and the respect the Greek community receives from the rest of the campus.

Drug Scene

The Lowdown On...
Drug Scene

Most Prevalent Drugs on Campus:

Alcohol

Marijuana

Liquor-Related Violations:

229

Drug-Related Violations:

91

Drug Counseling Programs:

The University Health Center offers classes, counseling, and psychological services to students. There's also a peer education group, Husker Choices, that educates students about alcohol.

Students Speak Out On...
Drug Scene

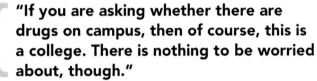

"If you are asking whether there are drugs on campus, then of course, this is a college. There is nothing to be worried about, though."

Q "Miniscule. I don't really think many people do drugs, although **Nebraska seems to have the most meth labs ever**, but if that is what you are into, you can always find them."

Q "It's there—**there are lots of drugs**, but I imagine it's no different than any other public university."

Q "I don't really know much about that. I'm sure it goes on, but **I'm just not aware of it**."

Q "There are not too many drugs, but I **have friends who do them (mostly weed)**. Most people who I know that do drugs have been caught or got into minor trouble because of them."

Q **"It is present** just like everywhere else."

Q "Well, if you're looking to score anything besides weed, good luck. Like I said before, don't do it in the dorms or the **campus police will make rounds on the floors of the dorms and they will bust you**."

Q "I don't really know. I'm sure that there is **someone in the dorms that does every drug in the book**, but you don't really hear that much about it."

Q "I am from Colorado, so I am used to a really large drug scene, and maybe it is just me but I did not notice it as much as I do at home. Maybe because all my friends at home do drugs, and not a lot at UNL. It is there, just like the drinking. I think **alcohol is easier to find** but just depends on what parties you hit."

Q I'm not very familiar with it, though there is obviously pot on campus. I will say that there is a **low incidence of date-rape drug reports on campus**. Our guys are not that bad after all."

Q "It's **pretty clean**, but every now and then, you have the pot smoker's floor and the wild dorm floor in Abel."

Q "There are **not too many drugs on campus**. The most prevalent one (and the only one I ever saw used) is marijuana."

Q "I don't know how to get them, but I think most people could if they tried. But it certainly **isn't prevalent and by no means the popular thing to do**."

The College Prowler Take On...
Drug Scene

For students with an itch to stretch the limits of their minds (and the law) it seems that weed is the drug of choice. Students say that the UNL campus is pretty tame when it comes to drugs, but there are ways to find what you seek. According to students, more serious drugs such as ecstasy and crystal meth aren't very prominent at UNL because neither a student's wallet nor grades can afford them.

There's an important difference between the drug scene in college and the drug scene in high school. In college, people do drugs because they want to and not because everybody else is doing it. You may not believe it yet, but students in college (or at least at UNL) will respect you more if you're your own person than if you follow the crowd. So, when it's your turn to take a hit, pass it on if you want because people won't judge you any differently than before.

A-

The College Prowler® Grade on

Drug Scene: A-

A high grade in the Drug Scene indicates that drugs are not a noticeable part of campus life; drug use is not visible, and no pressure to use them seems to exist.

Campus
Strictness

The Lowdown On...
Campus Strictness

What Are You Most Likely to Get Caught Doing on Campus?

- Being around alcohol (even if you're not drinking it)
- Breaking the speed limit
- Drinking alcohol (even if you're 21)
- Parking in the wrong spot
- Uploading music on Kazaa

Students Speak Out On...
Campus Strictness

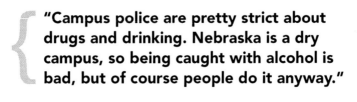

{ **"Campus police are pretty strict about drugs and drinking. Nebraska is a dry campus, so being caught with alcohol is bad, but of course people do it anyway."**

Q "They are really anal about it. Parties are always broken up off campus and drinking is easily detected in the dorms. **Police crack down hard and fast**."

Q "**The dorms have a 'no tolerance' drug and alcohol policy**. If you get caught, there are some severe penalties. All the Greek houses are supposed to be dry, too, but some of the frats find ways around it."

Q "They are **very strict in the dorms** if you are caught drinking or doing drugs, but if you don't have a strict RA on your floor, then you aren't likely to get caught."

Q "They are **getting more and more strict**, and it sucks."

Q "**You can get away with a lot**. In the dorms, it seems you can get by a little easier with those types of things. They will, however, crack down on the drugs."

Q "**Dorm life is strict** but outside of that, the world is your oyster."

Q "The party patrol busts all our off-campus parties. On campus, **if it's kept within your room no one will notice**."

Q "Since **Nebraska is a dry campus**, the campus police don't have much to do with drinking and such, since most people don't drink on campus, but instead go to off-campus parties. As far as city police, it is very rare for a person to get an MIP, because if a party does get busted up, the police just tell every one to put down their beer and leave."

Q "I have never been caught drinking on campus. Just be careful about doing it. If you get caught, you are not in huge trouble. Just be careful. The drugs, they are way, way stricter about. Do not do them on campus or **you will get caught**—it's a bad, bad idea."

Q "There are obviously rules against all these things, but it's not hard to get around them. There are much, much **stricter consequences for drugs then drinking**, however, and no one will tell you that you shouldn't drink. They'll just tell you not to drink on campus. If you want to do it, you'll find a way."

Q "They are getting to be **pretty strict here, especially with the fraternities**. One house lost its charter because of alcohol. Another was in big trouble because of a picture of alcohol and hazing in the basement of their house."

Q "UNL is a dry campus. If you **get busted with booze you have to take a class** and you get a fine."

Q "The campus police are **pretty lax about drinking as long as you don't drive** or do something to draw attention to yourself."

The College Prowler Take On...
Campus Strictness

To many students' great chagrin, the UNL campus is quite strict when it comes to its drug and alcohol policies. Students at UNL know the rules and they know how to bend them. Even students have their limits, however, and they say that breaking these limits is not worth the risk. If you do decide to drink on campus, be very cautious; but if you plan on doing drugs, you should either get as far away as possible, or get used to the sound of the police breaking down your door.

Campus isn't the only place in Lincoln that's strict. The Lincoln Police are very good at intruding on off-campus parties and they're even better at dishing out DUIs. So, be smart when you party because, chances are, you'll have to face the consequences if you're not.

The College Prowler® Grade on

Campus Strictness: C-

A high Campus Strictness grade implies an overall lenient atmosphere; police and RAs are fairly tolerant, and the administration's rules are flexible.

Parking

The Lowdown On...
Parking

UNL Parking Services:
(402) 472-1800
http://parking.unl.edu
park@cwis.unl.edu

Student Parking Lot?
Yes

Freshmen Allowed to Park?
Yes

Approximate Parking Permit Cost:
$171–$613 for nine months

Common Parking Tickets:

Expired Meter: $10

No Parking Zone: $30

Unauthorized Parking in a Reserved Area: $30

Handicapped Zone: $100

Fire Lane: $100

Parking Permits:

Red tag - faculty parking only

Blue tag - on-campus student parking

Green tag - off-campus student parking

Yellow tag - reserved lot student parking (expensive)

Gold tag - reserved garage student parking (expensive)

Purple tag - perimeter parking (cheap and good exercise)

Did You Know?

Best Places to Find a Parking Spot:
• The lots between 17th and 19th Streets

• Any of the three parking garages

Good Luck Getting a Parking Spot Here:
• Any street parking

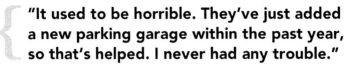

Students Speak Out On...
Parking

> "It used to be horrible. They've just added a new parking garage within the past year, so that's helped. I never had any trouble."

Q "Parking is expensive and **it sucks**."

Q "I've heard from transfer students that it **isn't as bad as other large universities**."

Q "The parking scene on campus is fair. It really depends on which dorm you live in. If you go to Nebraska I would recommend buying a blue parking permit, it offers the right amount of parking at a good price. Overall, it is **pretty easy to find a parking spot on campus**."

Q "Parking sucks. They **always sell way more passes than there are actually spots**—it sucks."

Q "**Parking is plentiful**, but you will only get the close spots if you buy a parking sticker. Freshmen, buy a pass for the blue lot."

Q "It sucks, even though they **just built a new parking garage**."

Q "**Parking can be quite the obstacle**. The University is notorious for selling more permits than there are spots so it can take quite some time to find a spot. Once you do, it can be quite a distance from where you're trying to get."

Q "They just built a brand new parking garage on campus last year. Before that, there was a parking problem, but now I don't hear people complain as much. The parking garage is extremely well lit and there are also **video cameras in all the rows**. I've never felt so safe in a parking garage."

Q "Parking on campus is **not as bad as they make it out** to be. You will never drive to class unless you drive to East Campus (about three miles away). There are parking garages and many lots close to the Greek row and all the dorms. Sometimes when I wanted to drive to a class I had on the edge of campus, I would drive downtown and park because it was closer than any of the campus parking. You won't have any classes over there unless you are architecture, interior design, or clothing textiles and design. So other than that, your classes will be close."

Q "Parking is pretty convenient. There are many good lots, but **it is kind of expensive**. There are different color-coded lots all over, but the most common is blue. That is what most freshmen choose. Sometimes it is hard to find a spot late at night or early in the morning, but for the most part you won't have trouble. Especially on the weekends when people go home."

Q "Parking pretty much sucks. They just built the second largest parking garage in the state right on campus, so that will be a huge help. There are big lots around and **you can always find a spot**—it's just that sometimes it takes awhile."

Q "The parking is pretty good compared to most other college campuses. Freshmen are allowed to bring their cars. I would **recommend buying the more expensive parking pass** (if you can afford it)."

Q "Don't think you can park in meters and get away from tickets. **Cops will ticket you**."

The College Prowler Take On...
Parking

Students are grateful for the new parking structures on campus. They also say that it's better compared to other places they have visited. Yet no student gave parking an enthusiastic two thumbs up, which means there are still improvements to be made.

It's fairly common to hear a student in class whine about how far they had to walk from their car. It may not be ideal, but UNL students are very privileged to have what they have. Freshmen are allowed to drive cars and there are enough spaces for everyone (even on the rare days when everyone actually shows up for class). Plus, the lots are well lit and patrolled around the clock to ensure the safety of you and your vehicle.

B-

The College Prowler® Grade on

Parking: B-

A high grade in the Parking section indicates that parking is both available and affordable, and that parking enforcement isn't overly severe.

Transportation

The Lowdown On...
Transportation

Ways to Get Around Town:

On Campus
Campus shuttle buses run every 15 minutes and also take students to East Campus.

Public Transportation
StarTran
(402) 476-1234
Schedules at the Student Union Information Desk.

Taxi Cabs
Capital Cab (402) 477-6074
Yellow Cab (402) 477-4111

Car Rentals
Avis
local: (402) 474-0001
national: (800) 331-1212
www.avis.com

Budget
local: (402) 467-2391
national: (800) 527-0700
www.budget.com

→

(Car rentals, continued)

Enterprise
local: (402) 488-2800
national: (800) 261-7331
www.enterprise.com

Hertz
local: (402) 474-4079
national: (800) 654-3131
www.hertz.com

National
local: (402) 474-4301
national: (800) 468-3334
www.nationalcar.com

Best Ways to Get Around Town

Get a car or get a friend because public transportation in Lincoln is fairly dismal. Biking is a popular alternative, but Nebraska weather tends to complicate things.

Ways to Get Out of Town:

Airport

Lincoln Airport

(402) 458-2480

www.lincolnairport.com

About 20 minutes from campus

Omaha Eppley Airfield

(402) 661-8000

www.eppleyairfield.com

About 80 minutes from campus

Airlines Serving Lincoln and Omaha

America West Airlines
(800) 235-9292
www.americawest.com

American Airlines
(800) 433-7300
www.aa.com

Continental
(800) 523-3273
www.continental.com

Delta
(800) 221-1212
www.delta-air.com

Frontier Airlines
(800) 432-1359
www.frontierairlines.com

Midwest Airlines
(800) 452-2022
www.midwestairlines.com

Northwest
(800) 225-2525
www.nwa.com

Southwest
(800) 435-9792
www.southwest.com

United
(800) 864-8331
www.united.com

How to Get to the Airport

Ask a friend

Take a cab (under $20)

Take OMALiNK, which travels between Lincoln and Omaha airports and costs (about $50)

www.omalink.com

Amtrak

The Amtrak station is about a mile away from campus in the Haymarket.

Lincoln Amtrak Train Station

201 N. 7th St.

(402) 476-1295
(800) 872-7245

www.amtrak.com

Greyhound

The Greyhound bus terminal is only a few blocks away from campus.

Lincoln Greyhound Bus Terminal

940 P St.

(402) 474-1041
(800) 231-2222

www.greyhound.com

Travel Agents

Travel Corner

4230 S. 33rd St.

(402) 441-5700

Omni Travel Inc.

4400 S. 70th St.

(402) 486-3300

Executive Travel

1212 O St.

(402) 483-2561

Students Speak Out On...
Transportation

"Public transportation is very convenient. Buses run all the time and in almost any route you would ever need."

"Not really convenient. They only have buses. They are sufficient on weekdays but on weekends, as usual, they run less. The **buses stop at around 6 p.m. on weekends** and 9 p.m. on weekdays—it can be a hassle."

"**There's a bus system that students ride for free**. However, it can be pretty crowded and take quite a while to get around."

"I've only used public transportation a couple of times because of the city-bus shuttles between campuses. It's not too bad, I guess. UNL students get free passes, which is cool. It **goes just about everywhere in the city**, and would be good, if you had the time."

"**UNL has its own bus system** and the city also has a very good bus system."

"You get a free bus pass on campus and a **free taxi ride when you're drunk**."

"In terms of campus, there's a shuttle that goes all over. I've never actually used it, but **there are stops in fairly convenient spots**, and I hear it's on time. If you get drunk and have your student ID on you, you can call 475-RIDE and get a free ride home. Other than that, there are other cabs here."

Q "You get a free bus pass for being a UNL student, so **it is really accessible**. And there are stops all over campus."

Q "We are given a bus pass and as long as we have our student ID we can ride free. There are shuttles that take you around campus, too. Plus, **taxis are pretty cheap and arrive quickly**."

Q "The public buses are convenient to get you between the East and City Campus, but as **for getting around the city, the transportation is not too great**."

The College Prowler Take On...
Transportation

UNL students really appreciate the free bus pass from the University, but that alone doesn't make the public transportation system work any better. UNL students also also take advantage of the free nightly taxi service the University provides to students who partied a little too hearty. Most of all, students rejoice in UNL's central location, which puts students within walking distance to most of their lifelines.

If you're from out-of-state or it's Spring Break and you want to get out-of-state, then be warned: the Lincoln airport is nothing spectacular. Always check the Omaha airport for better prices and more flexibility because it's offers more flight departures than Lincoln Municipal.

B

The College Prowler® Grade on

Transportation: B

A high grade for Transportation indicates that campus buses, public buses, cabs, and rental cars are readily-available and affordable. Other determining factors include proximity to an airport and the necessity of transportation.

Weather

The Lowdown On...
Weather

Average Temperature:

Fall: 54° F

Winter: 22° F

Spring: 51° F

Summer: 73° F

Average Precipitation:

Fall: 2.6 in.

Winter: 1.2 in.

Spring: 3.8 in.

Summer: 3.4 in.

Students Speak Out On...
Weather

"The winters are usually cold, windy, and snowy. The fall is very nice, especially with football season. The spring is mild and the summer is a little humid, but not too hot."

Q "It's **cold in the winter**! **Humid in the summer**, but not too bad."

Q "Horrible. When I first arrived in January, I thought I would **never thaw out after a Nebraskan winter**. It is so cold. Likewise, the summers are very hot. Luckily you only will have to endure the fall, winter, and spring. If you go to UNL, take warm clothes and don't forget your boots. Being from Colorado, known for the mountains, snow, ice and cold, I thought that Nebraska would be cake or equal. No! It is much colder. The humidity doesn't help."

Q "Well, the weather sucks. Today it was 96 and humid. In the winter it can be **negative 20 with 10 inches of snow** on the ground."

Q "I guess it depends on the year. This past winter, our big first snowfall (with enough to shovel) was in January and I think we only had that much two or three times. The year before, we seemed to have them nearly every week. I think the first one was in October. **Spring is nice, fall is great, and summer is hot**. We've been in the 90s for the past few days with a very high humidity percentage. I don't think about it much. I guess it's all in what you get used to."

Q "**Weather is about as varied as it gets** but you get used to it and learn to like the changes in climate. It was 83 degrees today and it will get warmer over the course of the summer. During the winter it can get very cold and snowy or it can be mild and not so bad."

Q "There are **warm summers**, and the winters have been cool, but not cold."

Q "**The weather leaves plenty to desire**. In the summer through late September it's hot and humid. It cools off in October and November, and it can get quite cold during the winter. We have been known to get a fair share of snow and ice. It frequently goes from extremes overnight. For example, one day it'll be 80 and sunny and the next it'll be in the mid 40s. You get used to it-kind of."

Q "**The weather changes a lot out here**. You can have to wear a coat and shorts in the same day."

Q "**The Midwest has crappy winters**. I am not going to lie! From about November to mid-April, it can be really cold one day and really nice the next. Lincoln has really weird weather—it really depends."

Q "The weather is typical for the plains—snowy cold winters, mild autumn, warm spring, hot summer. They think it's humid here, but it's not (Trust me, I came from Mississippi). This part of the country (Kansas, Nebraska, Oklahoma, Texas) **tends to have a lot of tornadoes in the summer**."

Q "We have a saying in Nebraska, '**If you don't like the weather, wait five minutes**.' It is absolutely true. I have lived here for 18 years and I can't figure out the weather."

Q "The weather is very, very odd. The temperature changes from negative degree temps in the winter to above 100 degrees in the summer. Also, the **temperatures in a single day are weird**. The low sometimes will be 35, but the high will be 75—it's kind of weird."

Q "Nice and cold in the winter, but when the weather gets nice, it is very pleasant. **Sometimes it snows and sometimes it just doesn't**—like this year."

Q "The weather is very windy on some days, but generally pretty nice. **We had a very mild winter**. The worst of the cold misses us because we are out of class for Christmas break. All in all, the weather is fairly nice."

Q "**Bring everything you own**—especially Husker clothing."

The College Prowler Take On...
Weather

The only students who chose UNL because of its weather are the meteorology majors who revel in chasing F-5 tornadoes. Students acknowledge that Nebraska weather is as varied and unpredictable as Madonna's latest look, and they've learned to adapt to its erratic nature.

Unfortunately, there are usually some weather patterns you can count on. Summer is sizzling—it's common for students to walk to their first week of classes in 100-degree heat. And winter is Arctic—one winter Lincoln recorded 12 days of sub-zero temperatures. The best solution to Lincoln's wide range of weather is to wake up in the morning prepared for anything. Always have a sweater for September and a pair of shorts for January, because there's no telling when you might need them.

The College Prowler® Grade on
Weather: C+

A high Weather grade designates that temperatures are mild and rarely reach extremes, that the campus tends to be sunny rather than rainy, and that weather is fairly consistent rather than unpredictable.

Report Card Summary

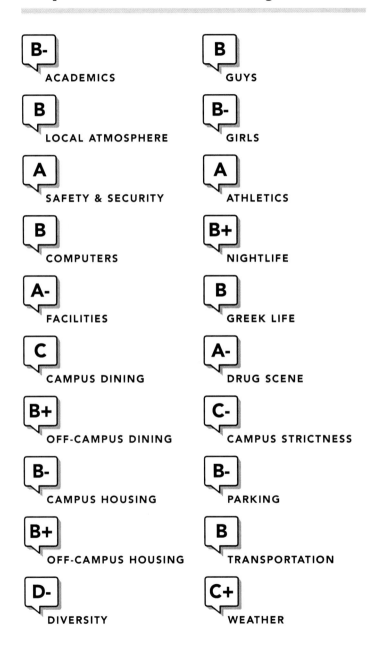

B-
ACADEMICS

B
GUYS

B
LOCAL ATMOSPHERE

B-
GIRLS

A
SAFETY & SECURITY

A
ATHLETICS

B
COMPUTERS

B+
NIGHTLIFE

A-
FACILITIES

B
GREEK LIFE

C
CAMPUS DINING

A-
DRUG SCENE

B+
OFF-CAMPUS DINING

C-
CAMPUS STRICTNESS

B-
CAMPUS HOUSING

B-
PARKING

B+
OFF-CAMPUS HOUSING

B
TRANSPORTATION

D-
DIVERSITY

C+
WEATHER

Overall Experience

Students Speak Out On...
Overall Experience

{ **"I truly love the University of Nebraska. It is a fine institution and I highly recommend it. The experience is one that I won't forget."**

Q "For a while, I wished I was somewhere else. I had a little trouble adjusting, but I really, really love it now. I wouldn't want to be anywhere else. **I would recommend Nebraska to anybody**. It is so much fun!"

Q "I love UNL. I came home for the summer and was miserable. I loved it sooo much I would go back to school right now, three weeks into summer. **I cannot imagine myself anywhere else**."

"I love it here, but **having it a little warmer would be a hell of a lot nicer**."

"Eventually, you realize that if you really try and make it work, **you can have a great college experience just about anywhere**."

"I love it. Probably because of all the **relationships I have made with my brothers**, but I love it. Sometimes, I wonder what it would be like at another school, but I'm happy here."

"I absolutely love UNL. I have no complaints whatsoever. I have made my best friends in the world here. The **atmosphere is great, the people are great, and the campus is beautiful**."

"Honestly, I love going to Lincoln. It is so much fun, the **atmosphere is great and everyone is friendly**."

"I really **wish I had gone somewhere else**."

"**I like this school a lot** and have many friends."

"I've had a good time. **I'm ready to graduate**, but that happens to everyone toward the end. I'll probably hang around Lincoln for a while, but who knows. I don't really have too many complaints. Overall, I've been happy here."

"It's okay. It's **all what you make it**."

"It's no Berkeley or Madison, but **we can still have fun**."

Q "My overall experience was a 7.5. Classes were fine, but **the youthful atmosphere could have been improved**. Join clubs right away and just get involved in everything. Yes, I do wish I were somewhere else. However, don't let me discourage you. UNL is a good place to go to school."

Q "The overall experience that I had at Nebraska was very good. I met **a lot of nice people and made a lot of friends**, which is really what made the experience for me."

Q "I absolutely **love UNL**."

The College Prowler Take On...
Overall Experience

Although it has its blemishes, most students just can't say enough the University of Nebraska. They love the atmosphere, they love the activities, and most of all they love the people that they have met here. The students here believe that almost any college can provide a great experience if you come to school with the right attitude and work ethic, and they agree that UNL is no different.

All in all, it is quite common for prospective students to put UNL on the back burner and place the more glamorous private schools first on their agendas. But, like myself, students eventually learn that Nebraska's academics and culture are almost the same as any other place. When it comes to good people and high spirits, there's really no other place like it.

The Inside Scoop

The Lowdown On...
The Inside Scoop

University of Nebraska Slang:

Know the slang, know the school. The following is a list of things you really need to know before coming to Nebraska. The more of these words you know, the better off you'll be.

Alphabet Sculpture – Tall red sculpture in front of CBA.

ASUN – Association of Students at the University of Nebraska (student government).

B-Dubs – Short for Buffalo Wild Wings (BW3's).

The Bells – Play at 25 minutes past every hour.

Blackboard – An online program that allows professors to post lecture notes and lets students e-mail people in their classes.

The Can-Man – A harmless homeless man who rides around campus on a bike collecting aluminum cans from the trash.

CASNR – College of Agricultural Sciences and Natural Resources.

→

CBA – College of Business Administration.

CLC – Chancellor's Leadership Class.

The Columns – Series of white stone columns between Memorial Stadium and the Coliseum.

CPN – Cather-Pound-Neihardt residence hall complex.

The Crib – Hangout by BK in the Union.

DN – The *Daily Nebraskan* is the school newspaper.

Elephant Hall - Morrill Hall, which has one of the world's leading collections of mammoth fossils.

E.N. Thompson Forum – A lecture series that attracts phenomenal speakers like Gorbacev, Maya Angelou, and Bono.

The Fountain – Geysers and rocks in front of the Student Union.

HSS – Harper-Schramm-Smith residence hall complex.

The Mall – The green space with fountains where 15th Street should be.

M&N – Military and Naval Science Building.

Nerdhardt – An appropriate nickname for Neihardt Residence Hall.

The Radiator – Nickname for Hamilton Hall, which looks like a 13-story radiator.

ROTC – Reserve Officer's Training Corps (Army, Marines, Navy, Air Force).

Smelleck – An appropriate nickname for Selleck Residence Hall.

Shmigos – Nickname for Amigos, a fast-food Mexican restaurant where students gorge themselves at 2 a.m.

Special K – Same tall red sculpture in front of CBA.

The Stacks – The short levels in Love Library.

The Torn Notebook – A sculpture of a giant spiral notebook.

Turd-foot – A sculpture by Architecture Hall that looks like a turd-molded foot.

UPC – University Program Council.

WAM – "What-About-Me" is the online program to register for classes or check your University bills.

Things I Wish I Knew Before Coming to the University of Nebraska

- There's more to college than a fancy dorm suite.
- Classes aren't all that bad here.
- If you're buying a computer, buy a laptop with wireless Internet capabilities. And while you're at it, save about five percent at the UNL Computer Store in the Student Union.
- Plan in advance if you want to study abroad.
- Study abroad.
- Find all the shortcuts, tunnels, and indoor walkways you can because your ears will be a lot less numb in January.
- Unless you're into burning money, don't park in a red zone.

Tips to Succeed at the University of Nebraska

- Join something but not everything.
- Drop by your prof's office and don't be shy.
- Living on campus is a great way to meet some great people.
- Join a summer program like NU Start or UNL Camp Bugeater to become more acquainted and comfortable with UNL and college.
- A recent UNL study found that students who go to the Rec Center have higher GPAs than students who don't.
- Explore Lincoln because there is a world off campus, too.
- Attend Big Red Welcome the Sunday night before classes start and get loads of information about what activities you can do at UNL. Plus, there are enough coupons to last you the rest of the semester.

University of Nebraska Urban Legends

The Temple Ghost

Dallas Williams, a former theater professor at UNL, died in 1971. The Temple Building, home to the UNL Theater Department, has allegedly been haunted by his ghost ever since.

The Columns

UNL has 24 white stone columns that reach toward the sky. People say that if a girl leaves UNL without ever hooking up, the columns will crash back down to earth.

The Collapsible Building

Hamilton Hall is made up of 13 unlucky floors of chemistry labs. It is built in three separate sections and many hypothesize that the divide was designed to keep two sections standing if a foolish student in lab goggles should happen to blow up the other one.

The Bell Tower

UNL's bell tower is much more than a source of entertainment and timekeeping. It's also one of campus' most notorious urban legends. In the era before cell phones, the bell caroler got locked inside the bell tower. He pounded on the door, but no one came to his rescue. Desperate, he began chiming the bells to the Beatles' tune, "Help." Eventually, someone went to see what all the playing was about and freed the caged caroler.

Newton's Apple Tree

You know the apple that dropped on Newton's head when he conceived gravity? Well, outside the physics building (Brace Hall) a direct descendant of Newton's apple tree is planted and inspires future discoveries at Nebraska.

The *Playboy* Staircase

The glass spiral staircase of Phi Delta Fraternity was once used as a backdrop for a *Playboy* photo shoot. There was some backlash, but the fraternity brothers didn't seem to mind.

School Spirit

There's one thing that unites the gym rats with the band geeks, the engineers with the English majors, and the frat brothers with the dormies—a Husker football Saturday. Even the students who don't own season tickets, however, are still Huskers. The school spirit is highly contagious and when you go to Nebraska your blood isn't just red—it's Husker red.

Traditions

The Cornhuskers
Formerly the Bugeaters, Tree Planters, and Rattlesnake Boys, the school finally settled on the Cornhuskers for its nickname.

"No Place Like It"
The school song, "No Place Like It," was written in 1920 by homesick ROTC officers at summer camp in Minnesota. Today, "There's No Place Like Nebraska" is the school motto.

The University Gates
In the late 1800s, a tall black-iron fence and four rounded gates enclosed the campus. When a main building on campus caught fire and the rescue team couldn't fit their trucks through the gates, the University removed the fencing. One gate remains and protects the entrance to the University's columns. As for the fence, it now borders Wyuka Cemetery at 40th and O Streets.

Homecoming
A week-long schedule of festivities, floats, and football is one of campus' largest traditions. Alumni flock back to campus as if it were Mecca and it's generally a good time had by all.

Memorial Stadium
Since 1962, there has not been an empty seat on a home game day at Memorial Stadium. That's more than 250 consecutive sellouts—more than any other college in the nation.

Ivy Day

Ivy Day celebrated its Centennial last year with the ceremonial planting of the ivy outside UNL's Love Library. The day marks the induction of the Black Masque Chapter of Mortar Board and UNL's own senior honor society, the Innocents.

Graduation

For some it comes too soon and for others it can't come soon enough. But for everyone, graduation is a special day. The speakers are average and the robes aren't very flattering, but there's one thing that separates UNL's graduation from almost every other university of its size. The Chancellor actually signs each student's diploma—not a machine, not a secretary, but the Chancellor himself.

Finding a Job or Internship

The Lowdown On...
Finding a Job or Internship

Besides the learning and partying of college, students go to UNL ultimately to get jobs. Through Career Services, located on the second floor of the Student Union, there are many resources on campus that can help students find a career path and then navigate through the employment maze.

Advice

Many students dart off to career fairs and advising sessions when they want to learn more about jobs and internships. That's a good start, but don't forget about one of the most valuable assets the University has to offer you a wise and well-connected professor. Find a professor you like, take all his/her classes, really get to know them and listen to what they have to say because they are the best guides to your future.

Career Center Resources & Services

Career fairs, Career Week, choosing majors, matching careers, Dining Etiquette Seminar, employer information sessions, Graduate and Professional School Expo, insights into internships, Internship Orientation Session, interview tips, jobsearch survival, Networking Workshop, Professional Development Day(s), resume and cover letter advising, Web data about jobs and internships

Firms That Most Frequently Hire Grads:

Archer-Daniels Midland, Deloitte & Touche, Goodyear, Lincoln Public Schools, Olsson Associates, Omaha Public Schools

Grads Who Enter the Job Market Within

6 Months: 36%

1 Year: N/A

Average Salary Information

The following statistics represent average starting salaries for University of Nebraska graduates by major. If the information for a specific major does not exist, no one from that major reported back.

Accounting	$35,006
Actuarial Science	$50,571
Advertising	$33,750
Agribusiness	$37,429
Agricultural Economics	$30,000
Agricultural Education	$39,500
Agricultural Engineering	$47,333
Agronomy	$24,000
Animal Science	$30,682
Anthropology	$26,333
Architectural Studies	$29,333
Art	$26,500
Biochemistry	$23,407
Biological Sciences	$28,333
Biological Systems Engineering	$52,250
Broadcasting	$17,900
Business Administration	$33,163
Business Ed./Cooperative Ed.	$27,500
Chemical Engineering	$47,800
Civil Engineering	$40,971
Communication Studies	$32,777
Community Health Education	$37,500
Computer Engineering	$44,900
Computer Science	$41,813
Construction Management	$45,531
Criminal Justice	$33,000
Dental Hygiene	$37,373
Diversified Agricultural	$34,318
Economics	$34,600
Electrical Engineering	$49,364
Elementary Education	$29,506

English	$30,333
Environmental Studies	$27,833
Exercise Science	$35,833
Finance	$34,679
Fisheries and Wildlife	$31,333
History	$20,667
Horticulture	$26,667
Industrial Engineering	$46,165
Interior Design	$30,000
International Business	$39,250
International Studies	$30,000
Management	$33,714
Marketing	$34,148
Mathematics	$37,944
Mechanical Engineering	$48,916
Mechanized Systems Management	$39,250
Merchandising	$23,500
Meteorology/Climatology	$29,000
Middle Grades Education	$27,000
Music	$30,520
Music Education	$27,402
Natural Science	$24,333
News and Editorial	$25,133
Nursing	$40,137
Political Science	$31,500
Psychology	$30,250
Social Science	$30,272
Sociology	$31,000
Spanish	$37,000
Veterinary Science	$32,000

Alumni

The Lowdown On...
Alumni

Web Site:

www.huskeralum.com

Office:

Wick Alumni Center

1520 R St.
Lincoln, NE 68501

(402) 472-2841

(888) 353-1874

Alumni Publications:

Nebraska Magazine comes out four times a year and reaches 32,000 alumni. Members of the Alumni Association receive the publication as a benefit of membership.

Major Alumni Events

Homecoming
Thousands of alumni flock back to campus each year for Homecoming. The main event, of course, is the football game, but there are tons of other festivities on and around campus.

Master's Week
Five alumni are annually selected as "Masters." These graduates have excelled in their fields or accomplished something special. To reward them, the Alumni Association hosts an entire week of lectures, dinners, and ceremonies in their honor.

Services Available

Tourin' Huskers
Every year, the Alumni Association organizes trips around the world for Nebraska alums to participate in.

Alumni Career Network
The ACN helps alumni make connections with other Nebraska alumni in the business world.

Football Tours
Whenever the Huskers are on the road, so is the Alumni Association. The events and accommodations are all taken care of, which makes for a pretty easy weekend getaway.

Husker Huddle
Whenever the Huskers play a home game, the Alumni Association hosts a large pre-game tailgate for alumni, friends, and family.

Did You Know?

Famous University of Nebraska Alumni:

John J. Pershing (Class of 1893) - army general in World War I

Willa Cather (Class of 1895) - author of *My Antonia* and *O Pioneers!*

Aaron Douglas (Class of 1922) - a leader of the Harlem Renaissance

Ted Hustead (Class of 1929) - founder of Wall Drug

Johnny Carson (Class of 1949) - host of NBC's *Tonight Show*

Warren Buffett (Class of 1950) - One of the 10 wealthiest men in the world

Student Organizations

The University of Nebraska has tons of recognized student organizations that range from equestrians to evangelists. To find more about a certain student organization, go to *http://einvolvement.unl.edu.*

Abel Residence Association

Abundant Life

Actuarial Science Club

Advertising Club

Afghan Renascent Youth Association

Afghan Student Association

African Student Association

Afrikan Peoples Union

Agricultural Communicators of Tomorrow (ACT)

Agricultural Economics/ Agribusiness Club

Agricultural Education Club/ Alpha Tau Alpha

Agricultural Leadership, Education & Communication Graduate Student Association

Agronomy and Horticulture Graduate Student Association (AGSA)

Agronomy Club

Allies and Advocates for GLBT Equality

Alpha Epsilon Delta

Alpha Kappa Psi - Professional Business Fraternity

Alpha Lambda Delta

Alpha Omega Campus Ministry

Alpha Phi Omega

Alpha Phi Sigma

Alpha Pi Mu

Alpha Rho Chi
(Pytheos Chapter)

Alpha Zeta

Amateur Radio Club, UNL

Ambassadors, University

American Association of
Family & Consumer Sciences

American Association of
Petroleum Geologists,
Student Chapter

American Association of
Textile Chemists

American Cancer Society,
UNL Chapter

American Chemical Society

American Guild of Organists

American Institute of
Architecture Students

American Institute of
Chemical Engineers (AIChE)

American Marketing
Association

American Meteorological
Society

American Society of
Agricultural Engineers (ASAE)

American Society of Civil
Engineers

American Society of Interior
Designers (ASID)

American Society of
Mechanical Engineers (ASME)

American String Teachers
Association Student Chapter

Amnesty International

Animal Science Graduate
Student Association

Anthro Group

Arnold Air Society

Art League

Arts & Sciences Student
Advisory Board

Asian Student Alliance (ASA)

ASM International-American
Society of Metals

Associated General
Contractors

Associated Landscape
Contractors of America

Association for
Computing Machinery

Association for
Independent Music

Association for India's
Development Nebraska
Chapter

Astronomy Club, UNL

ASUN (Association of
Students of the University
of Nebraska)

Baha'i Student Association

Ballroom Dance Club

Baseball Club

Bathtub Dogs

Berean College Group

Beta Alpha Psi (Delta
Omicron Chapter)

Beta Gamma Sigma

Bible Study Club

Big Red Objectivist Club

Bigs on Campus (BOC)

Biochemistry Club

Biological Chemistry
Graduate Student Association

Biological Graduate Student
Association

Biology Club

Biomedical Engineering
Society

Black Graduate
Student Association

Black Law
Student Association

Block and Bridle Club

Burr-Fedde Association of
Resident Members

Campus Advent

Campus Crusade for Christ

Campus Freethought Alliance

Campus Recreation Advisory
Council

Campus Red Cross

CASNR Week Program
Council

Cather Pound Residence
Association

Chapter of the Lutheran
Student Movement,
University of Nebraska

Chess Club, UNL

Chi Epsilon

Chinese Language & Cultural
Exchange Association

Chinese Student & Scholar
Association

Christian Challenge

Christian Legal Society

Christian Medical Dental
Association (CMDA)

Christian Student Fellowship

Christians at UNL

Cinema 16

Circle K

Clay Club

Climbing Club

College Libertarians of UNL

College of Agricultural
Sciences & Natural Resources
Advisory Board (CASNR)

College of Business
Administration Student
Advisory Board

College of Education &
Human Sciences
Advisory Board

College of Engineering
and Technology Student
Advisory Board

College Republicans

Collegiate 4-H

Collegiate Entrepreneurs
Organization

Collegiate Music Educators
National Conference

Communication Studies
Club, UNL

Conventus Classicus

Counseling Psychology
Student Organization

Crew Club

Criminal Justice Student
Association

Culinology & Restaurant
Management Club

Cultural Ambassadors
Program (CA)

Culture Center
Coalition (CCC)

Cycling Club

Czech Komensky
(Comenius) Club

Daily Nebraskan

Dance Marathon

Day Trippers Photo Club

Delta Epsilon Chi

Delta Sigma Pi

Delta Theta Phi Law Fraternity

Design-Build Institute of America

Diverse Student Association

Diversified Ag Club

Diversity Enhancement Team (DET)

Division of General Studies Student Advisory Board

Dodgeball Club

Ducks Unlimited Chapter, UNL

Eating Disorders Education and Prevention (EDEP)

Ecology Now

Economics Graduate Student Association

Educational Administration Graduate Student Association

Egyptian Students Organization

Engineers Without Frontiers

English Graduate Student Association (EGSA)

Environmental Resource Center

Equal Justice Society

Equestrian Team, UNL

Eta Kappa Nu (HKN)

Federalist Society for Law & Public Policy Studies

Fellowship of Catholic University Students (FOCUS)

Fellowship of Christian Athletes

FFA Alumni Association

Finance Club

Floor Hockey Club Enduring Rigorous Studies

Flying Huskers Booster Club

Food Science Club

Forensics Team/Forensics Union, Affiliated with Delta Sigma Rho-Tau Kappa Alpha

Foto UNL

Friends of The Deaf Community

Game Developers Club

Gamers Association

Gamma Theta Upsilon (Alpha Phi Chapter)

Geography Student Organization

Geology Club

Geosciences Graduate Student Association

Global Friends of Japan

Golden Key International Honor Society

Graduate House Government Council

Graduate Women in Science

Greek Ambassadors

Green Party of UNL

Habitat for Humanity, UNL

Handball Club

Harper Schramm Smith Residence Association

Hillel /Jewish Student Association

History Graduate Student's Association

Hixson-Lied College of Fine & Performing Arts Advisory Board

Hockey Club

Honors Ambassadors

Honors Program Student Advisory Board

Horticulture Club

Humanities in Medicine

Husker Choices

Husker Hall Residence Association

Husker Linux Users Group

Husker Village Council

Huskers Against Hergert (HAH)

Indian Students Association

Inform

Innocents Society

Insect Science Club

Institute of Electrical & Electronics Engineering (IEEE)

Institute of Industrial Engineers

Institute of Transportation Engineers

Intelligent Design and Evolution Awareness Club

Interfraternity Council

International Association for the Exchange of Students for Technical Experience (IAESTE)

International Folk Dancers

International Pageant Association (IPA)

International Student Organization

Intervarsity Christian Fellowship

Iranian Students Organization of Nebraska (ISON)

Italian Club

J. Reuben Clark Law Society

Jones Scholars Alumni

Journalism and Mass Communication Student Advisory Board

Judo Club

Juggling Club

Kappa Kappa Psi

Kauffman Residents' Association

Korean Student Association

Kreate 4 Kidz

Latter Day Saint Student Association

Laurus Magazine

Leadership Advantage

Learning Communities, University of NE.

Lincoln Fantasy and Science Fiction Club

Lincoln Friends of Foreign Students: Student Workteam Organization

Lincoln Nights

Lions Club

Love Memorial Hall Cooperative

Lutheran Chapel

Management Information Systems Club

Masters of Business Administration (MBA) Student Association

Mechanical/Electrical Specialty Contractors

Mechanized Systems Management Club

Men's Lacrosse

Men's Rugby Club

Men's Soccer Club

Mexican American Student Association (MASA)

Minorities in Agricultural Natural Resources and Related Sciences (MANRRS)

Mock Trial Club

Montage

Mortar Board

Mu Phi Epsilon (International Prof. Music Fraternity)

Mudwrestling Organization

Multicultural Greek Council

Multicultural Legal Society

Music Teachers National Association, Collegiate Chapter University of Nebraska Lincoln

Muslim Students Association

National Agri-Marketing Association (NAMA)

National Association of Home Builders - Student Chapter

National Broadcasting Society (NBS)

National Pan-Hellenic Council

National Residence Hall Honorary

National Society of Black Engineers

National Society of Collegiate Scholars, The

National Student Speech, Language and Hearing Association (NSSLHA)

Navigators, The

Nebraska Association of Sociology Graduate Students

Nebraska Association of Student Councils (NASC) Staffers at UNL

Nebraska Blueprint

Nebraska Bowling Team

Nebraska Educators Really Doing Science (NERDS)

Nebraska Entertainment and Sports Law Association

Nebraska International Multi-Cultural Student Association (NIMSA)

Nebraska Leadership Seminar, Inc. Alumni Association

Nebraska Masquers

Nebraska Model United Nations

Nebraska Student Dental Association

Nebraska Students For Young Children

Nebraska Union Billiards Club

Nebraska Union Board

Nebraska University Mac User Group (NUMUG)

Nebraska University Malaysian Student Association (NUMSA)

Nebraskans for Peace

Nebraskans for the Upgraded Treatment of Squirrels

Neihardt Council

Newman Center

NROTC/Naval Reserve Officer Training Corps Battalion Recreational Council

NU ANTS

NU Connections Peer Mentors

NU Life

NU Meds

NU Start Advisory Board / NU Start Summer Program

Nutrition & Health Promotion Association

Omicron Delta Epsilon

Omicron Delta Kappa

One Body

Optical Society of America, Student Chapter

Orchesis

Order Of Omega

Orthodox Christian Fellowship

Otaku Jinrui: The UNL Anime Club

Outdoor Adventure Club

Pagan Life

Paintball Club

Pakistan Students Association

Panhellenic Association

Permias Indonesian Student Association

Pershing Rifles Company A-2

Pershing Rifles National Headquarters

Phi Alpha Delta Fraternity, International Pre-Law

Phi Beta Delta

Phi Beta Lambda

Phi Delta Gamma, Tau Chapter

Phi Eta Sigma

Phi Kappa Theta Affiliate

Phi Sigma Pi-National Honors Fraternity

Phi Theta Kappa Alumni Association

Phi Upsilon Omicron

Physicians Assistants, NU

Pi Alpha Xi (Alpha Gamma Chapter)

Pi Lambda Theta

Pi Mu Epsilon

Pi Sigma Alpha

Pi Tau Sigma

Plant Pathology Student Organization

Poker Club, UNL

Pre-Dental Club

Pre-Health Club

Pre-Law Club

Pre-Optometry Club

Pre-Pharmacy

Pre-Physical Therapy Club

Pre-Veterinary Club

PREVENT: Agents of Change

Professional Golf Management Club (PGM)

PROTECT

Psi Chi

Public Relations Student Society of America

Queer Student Alliance

RAAG

Range Management Club

Reformed University Fellowship

Republican Law Students Association

Residence Hall Association (RHA)

Rifle Club

Rodeo Association

Runners Club

Russian Club

Sandoz Hall Council

Scarlett Keep Medieval Recreation Society

School of Natural Resources Graduate Student Association

Selleck Quadrangle Residence Council

Semper Fidelis Society

Shotokan Karate of America Club

Sigma Alpha Iota

Sigma Delta Pi

Sigma Lambda Beta - Phi Alpha

Sigma Lambda Chi

Sigma Lambda Gamma

Sigma Psi Zeta Sorority, Inc.

Silver Wings Chapter at the University of Nebraska-Lincoln

Singapore Club@Nebraska

Ski and Snowboard Team

SkillsUSA Nebraska

Society for Human Resource Management

Society of Automotive Engineers (SAE)

Society of Physics Students

Society of Women Engineers

Soil and Water Resources Club

Sport Club Council

Sports Officials Association

Sri-Lanka Association

Student Advocates for Academic Freedom

Student Agribusiness Masters of Business Administration Club

Student Alumni Association

Student Athlete Advisory Committee

Student Athletic Training Organization

Student Council for Exceptional Children

Student Education Association

Student Foundation, UNL

Student Nurses Association, UNL

Student Organization Representatives to the Athletic Department (SORAD)

Student Planning Association of Nebraska (SPAN)

Student Support and Services Advisory Board

Student Technology Training

Student Turf Club, UNL

Student Undergraduate Middle Level Organization

Students for Choice

Students for Life

Students For Responsible Business

Students in Free Enterprise (SIFE)

Students Taking Action for Human Rights (STAHR)

SWAT Team

Swimming Club

Synchronized Swimming

Tabernacle of Grace for all Nations Christian Fellowship

Table Tennis Club

Tae Kwon Do

Taiji Martial Arts Association

Taiwanese Student Association

Tau Beta Pi

Tau Sigma

Tau Sigma Delta

Tennis Club

Thai Association of University of Nebraska (TANU)

Tobacco Education Advocacy Mentors

Towne Club

Training in Relationships and Educating in Abstinence

Turkish Student Association (TSA)

Ultimate Frisbee

Undergraduate English Organization

Undergraduate Psychology Organization

Undergraduate Sociology Association

Undergraduate Women in Business

UNITE (University of Nebraska Inter-Tribal Exchange)

University Chorale

University Health Center Advisory Board

University Program Council (UPC)

UNL Students for Kucinich

Varsity Men's Chorus

Vietnamese Student Association (VSA)

Visual Artists in Practice (VAP)

Walt Disney World College Program Alumni Association, UNL Chapter

Water Environment Federation-Water Works

Water Polo Club

Wildlife Club

Women's Lacrosse

Women's Rugby

Women's Soccer Club

Women's Studies Association

Women's Undergraduate Mathematics Network (WUMN)

Women's Volleyball Club

Won By One Christian Fellowship

Wrestling Spirit Leaders

Xtreme Devotion (Chi Alpha Christian Fellowship)

Yard Association for Residential Development, The (Yard)

Young Democrats

Young Life

Your Degree First

The Best & Worst

The Ten **BEST** Things About Nebraska

1	Happy people
2	Championship athletics and a winning school spirit
3	Big school with a small-school feel
4	University Program Council events
5	Undergraduate research opportunities
6	Safety
7	Lied Center for Performing Arts
8	You get the true college experience here
9	Beautiful campus
10	Terrific professors

The Ten WORST Things About Nebraska

1	Nebraska winters
2	Nebraska summers
3	Parking
4	Lack of diversity
5	Not considered "prestigious"
6	Not-so-hot shopping
7	Leftover cafeteria food
8	Squirrels
9	Too much construction
10	Apathetic professors

Visiting

The Lowdown On...
Visiting

Hotel Information:

Some hotels may offer a discount to campus visitors. To see if a discount is available, mention your University of Nebraska campus visit at the time of reservation.

For other locations please contact Lincoln Lodging at (402) 434-5334 or the Lincoln Visitors Bureau at *www.lincoln. org/cvb/lodging/lodging.htm*

AmericInn Lodge
6555 N. 27th St.
(800) 634-3444
Distance from Campus: 5 miles
Price Range: $85 and up

Baymont Inn & Suites
3939 N. 26th St.
(402) 477-1100
Distance from Campus: 4–5 miles
Price Range: $50–$73

→

The Cornhusker, Marriott

333 S. 13th St.

(402) 474-7474
(800) 793-7474

www.marriott.com

Distance from Campus:
Less than 1 mile

Price Range: $129–$149

Embassy Suites

1040 P St.

(402) 474-1111
(800) EMBASSY

www.embassysuites.com

Distance from Campus:
Less than 1 mile

Price Range: $104–$149

Holiday Inn

141 N. 9th St

(402) 475-4011
(800) HOLIDAY

www.holiday-inn.com

Distance from Campus:
Less than 1 mile

Price Range: $71–$141
(mention discount code U11)

Ramada Limited North

4433 N. 27th St.

(402) 476-2222
(800) 2-RAMADA

www.ramada.com

Distance from Campus: 5 miles

Price Range: $60–$70

Staybridge Suites by Holiday Inn

2701 Fletcher Ave.

(402) 438-7829
(800) 238-8000

*www.staybridge.com/
lincolni-80*

Distance from Campus:
2–3 miles

Price Range: $69–$125

Take a Campus Virtual Tour

www.unl.edu/unlpub/tour/frame3/index_fullpage.shtml

To Schedule a Group Information Session or Interview

Call (800) 742-8800 ext. 4887, e-mail: visit.us@unl.edu, or visit *http://admissions.unl.edu/dailyvisit.*

Campus Tours

Daily campus visits are available Monday through Friday and on selected Saturdays. Saturday visits include a general information session and a tour of campus. Appointments with academic programs or with the Scholarships & Financial Aid Office are only available Monday–Friday. During the summer, we recommend the morning session because of the extreme temperatures. However, we still offer both sessions. Contact us in advance to ensure the availability of a tour.

Red Letter Days and NU Previews are big events with many prospective students and are great days to get a dose of UNL life. Red Letter Days are for high school seniors and NU Previews are for high school juniors. To find out dates and more specifics, visit *http://admissions.unl.edu/rld/index.asp.*

Overnight Visits

Not available

Directions to Campus

From the North

• Take Highway 77 South to I-80. Follow "From I-80" directions listed below.

From I-80

• Take I-80 to the Downtown exit (401A) going south.
• Turn left on P Street and continue on to 17th Street.
• Turn left on 17th to Q Street Turn left on Q.
• Go 1.5 blocks west on Q and park in the visitor lot east of the Alexander Building.

From The South (Highway 2)

• Continue on Highway 2 as it wraps around town to the West. It will turn into 10th Street.
• Continue on 10th and turn right on P Street.
• Continue on P Street to 17th Street.
• Turn left onto 17th and then onto Q Street.
• Go 1.5 blocks west on Q and park in the visitor lot east of the Alexander Building.

From the South (Highway 77)

• Take Highway 77 North to Capitol Parkway.
• Turn right on Capitol Parkway (K Street), then turn left on 17th Street.
• Continue on 17th Street to Q Street Turn left on Q Street.
• Go 1.5 blocks west on Q and park in the visitor lot east of the Alexander Building.

Words to Know

Academic Probation – A suspension imposed on a student if he or she fails to keep up with the school's minimum academic requirements. Those unable to improve their grades after receiving this warning can face dismissal.

Beer Pong/Beirut – A drinking game involving cups of beer arranged in a pyramid shape on each side of a table. The goal is to get a ping pong ball into one of the opponent's cups by throwing the ball or hitting it with a paddle. If the ball lands in a cup, the opponent is required to drink the beer.

Bid – An invitation from a fraternity or sorority to 'pledge' (join) that specific house.

Blue-Light Phone – Brightly-colored phone posts with a blue light bulb on top. These phones exist for security purposes and are located at various outside locations around most campuses. In an emergency, a student can pick up one of these phones (free of charge) to connect with campus police or a security escort.

Campus Police – Police who are specifically assigned to a given institution. Campus police are typically not regular city officers; they are employed by the university in a full-time capacity.

Club Sports – A level of sports that falls somewhere between varsity and intramural. If a student is unable to commit to a varsity team but has a lot of passion for athletics, a club sport could be a better, less intense option. Even less demanding, intramural (IM) sports often involve no traveling and considerably less time.

Cocaine – An illegal drug. Also known as "coke" or "blow," cocaine often resembles a white crystalline or powdery substance. It is highly addictive and dangerous.

Common Application – An application with which students can apply to multiple schools.

Course Registration – The period of official class selection for the upcoming quarter or semester. Prior to registration, it is best to prepare several back-up courses in case a particular class becomes full. If a course is full, students can place themselves on the waitlist, although this still does not guarantee entry.

Division Athletics – Athletic classifications range from Division I to Division III. Division IA is the most competitive, while Division III is considered to be the least competitive.

Dorm – A dorm (or dormitory) is an on-campus housing facility. Dorms can provide a range of options from suite-style rooms to more communal options that include shared bathrooms. Most first-year students live in dorms. Some upperclassmen who wish to stay on campus also choose this option.

Early Action – An application option with which a student can apply to a school and receive an early acceptance response without a binding commitment. This system is becoming less and less available.

Early Decision – An application option that students should use only if they are certain they plan to attend the school in question. If a student applies using the early decision option and is admitted, he or she is required and bound to attend that university. Admission rates are usually higher among students who apply through early decision, as the student is clearly indicating that the school is his or her first choice.

Ecstasy – An illegal drug. Also known as "E" or "X," ecstasy looks like a pill and most resembles an aspirin. Considered a party drug, ecstasy is very dangerous and can be deadly.

Ethernet – An extremely fast Internet connection available in most university-owned residence halls. To use an Ethernet connection properly, a student will need a network card and cable for his or her computer.

Fake ID – A counterfeit identification card that contains false information. Most commonly, students get fake IDs with altered birthdates so that they appear to be older than 21 (and therefore of legal drinking age). Even though it is illegal, many college students have fake IDs in hopes of purchasing alcohol or getting into bars.

Frosh – Slang for "freshman" or "freshmen."

Hazing – Initiation rituals administered by some fraternities or sororities as part of the pledging process. Many universities have outlawed hazing due to its degrading, and sometimes dangerous, nature.

Intramurals (IMs) – A popular, and usually free, sport league in which students create teams and compete against one another. These sports vary in competitiveness and can include a range of activities—everything from billiards to water polo. IM sports are a great way to meet people with similar interests.

Keg – Officially called a half-barrel, a keg contains roughly 200 12-ounce servings of beer.

LSD – An illegal drug, also known as acid, this hallucinogenic drug most commonly resembles a tab of paper.

Marijuana – An illegal drug, also known as weed or pot; along with alcohol, marijuana is one of the most commonly-found drugs on campuses across the country.

Major –The focal point of a student's college studies; a specific topic that is studied for a degree. Examples of majors include physics, English, history, computer science, economics, business, and music. Many students decide on a specific major before arriving on campus, while others are simply "undecided" until declaring a major. Those who are extremely interested in two areas can also choose to double major.

Meal Block – The equivalent of one meal. Students on a meal plan usually receive a fixed number of meals per week. Each meal, or "block," can be redeemed at the school's dining facilities in place of cash. Often, a student's weekly allotment of meal blocks will be forfeited if not used.

Minor – An additional focal point in a student's education. Often serving as a complement or addition to a student's main area of focus, a minor has fewer requirements and prerequisites to fulfill than a major. Minors are not required for graduation from most schools; however some students who want to explore many different interests choose to pursue both a major and a minor.

Mushrooms – An illegal drug. Also known as "'shrooms," this drug resembles regular mushrooms but is extremely hallucinogenic.

Off-Campus Housing – Housing from a particular landlord or rental group that is not affiliated with the university. Depending on the college, off-campus housing can range from extremely popular to non-existent. Students who choose to live off campus are typically given more freedom, but they also have to deal with possible subletting scenarios, furniture, bills, and other issues. In addition to these factors, rental prices and distance often affect a student's decision to move off campus.

Office Hours – Time that teachers set aside for students who have questions about coursework. Office hours are a good forum for students to go over any problems and to show interest in the subject material.

Pledging – The early phase of joining a fraternity or sorority, pledging takes place after a student has gone through rush and received a bid. Pledging usually lasts between one and two semesters. Once the pledging period is complete and a particular student has done everything that is required to become a member, that student is considered a brother or sister. If a fraternity or a sorority would decide to "haze" a group of students, this initiation would take place during the pledging period.

Private Institution – A school that does not use tax revenue to subsidize education costs. Private schools typically cost more than public schools and are usually smaller.

Prof – Slang for "professor."

Public Institution – A school that uses tax revenue to subsidize education costs. Public schools are often a good value for in-state residents and tend to be larger than most private colleges.

Quarter System (or Trimester System) – A type of academic calendar system. In this setup, students take classes for three academic periods. The first quarter usually starts in late September or early October and concludes right before Christmas. The second quarter usually starts around early to mid–January and finishes up around March or April. The last academic quarter, or "third quarter," usually starts in late March or early April and finishes up in late May or Mid-June. The fourth quarter is summer. The major difference between the quarter system and semester system is that students take more, less comprehensive courses under the quarter calendar.

RA (Resident Assistant) – A student leader who is assigned to a particular floor in a dormitory in order to help to the other students who live there. An RA's duties include ensuring student safety and providing assistance wherever possible.

Recitation – An extension of a specific course; a review session. Some classes, particularly large lectures, are supplemented with mandatory recitation sessions that provide a relatively personal class setting.

Rolling Admissions – A form of admissions. Most commonly found at public institutions, schools with this type of policy continue to accept students throughout the year until their class sizes are met. For example, some schools begin accepting students as early as December and will continue to do so until April or May.

Room and Board – This figure is typically the combined cost of a university-owned room and a meal plan.

Room Draw/Housing Lottery – A common way to pick on-campus room assignments for the following year. If a student decides to remain in university-owned housing, he or she is assigned a unique number that, along with seniority, is used to determine his or her housing for the next year.

Rush – The period in which students can meet the brothers and sisters of a particular chapter and find out if a given fraternity or sorority is right for them. Rushing a fraternity or a sorority is not a requirement at any school. The goal of rush is to give students who are serious about pledging a feel for what to expect.

Semester System – The most common type of academic calendar system at college campuses. This setup typically includes two semesters in a given school year. The fall semester starts around the end of August or early September and concludes before winter vacation. The spring semester usually starts in mid-January and ends in late April or May.

Student Center/Rec Center/Student Union – A common area on campus that often contains study areas, recreation facilities, and eateries. This building is often a good place to meet up with fellow students; depending on the school, the student center can have a huge role or a non-existent role in campus life.

Student ID – A university-issued photo ID that serves as a student's key to school-related functions. Some schools require students to show these cards in order to get into dorms, libraries, cafeterias, and other facilities. In addition to storing meal plan information, in some cases, a student ID can actually work as a debit card and allow students to purchase things from bookstores or local shops.

Suite – A type of dorm room. Unlike dorms that feature communal bathrooms shared by the entire floor, suites offer bathrooms shared only among the suite. Suite-style dorm rooms can house anywhere from two to ten students.

TA (Teacher's Assistant) – An undergraduate or grad student who helps in some manner with a specific course. In some cases, a TA will teach a class, assist a professor, grade assignments, or conduct office hours.

Undergraduate – A student in the process of studying for his or her bachelor's degree.

ABOUT THE AUTHOR

It's hard to believe, but after three years and five majors I'll be entering my senior year at UNL. Today I'm an advertising major, but I have no idea what or where I'll be tomorrow. Whatever I do in the future, I hope it involves writing and a concoction of the real-life skills I picked up at the University. As for now, I'm learning how to play the guitar, managing a legislature campaign, and visiting my friends and family every chance I get.

And now for my long-winded Oscar speech. I'm very grateful to College Prowler for the opportunity to say, "I wrote the book on the University of Nebraska." I'd also like to thank my parents for cheering me on since before I could even remember, every person who ever taught me to love sentences, especially my Morrie, Gerry Shapiro, the supremely fabulous Stacy James, Lisa Lyons, who though she won't agree, is to UNL what superglue is to a model car, Annie Magnusson, Joan Kunzman, Kelley Winter, and Marsha Fortney for making it so easy to love my job, Camilo, Ian, and Adam-Cather 12 and The Omaha Mining Company forever, Erica and Caitlin for the longest, loveliest friendships of my life, Troy and Jill for consulting me on Lincoln nightlife because I'm only 20, and all my other amazing friends who are the reason I get tingles even on my ankles whenever I think about how much I've loved my time at Nebraska—Marie Joelle, Jon, Jonn, John, Jonathan B, Emily C, Emily H, Emily H2, Nick, Brittany, Joey, Jesse, Jaron, Eric, Steve, Jeannine, Catherine, Kelsey, Maggie, Sarah H, Carrie J, AJ, Melissa, Val2000, Elaination, Jill G, Katie W, Megan W, and Anna Dom. Cue the orchestra, I think I'm done.

Aaron Eske
aaroneske@collegeprowler.com

California Colleges

California dreamin'?
This book is a must have for you!

CALIFORNIA COLLEGES
7¼" X 10", 762 Pages Paperback
$29.95 Retail
1-59658-501-3

Stanford, UC Berkeley, Caltech—California is home
to some of America's greatest institutes of higher
learning. *California Colleges* gives the lowdown on 24
of the best, side by side, in one prodigious volume.

New England Colleges

Looking for peace in the Northeast?
Pick up this regional guide to New England!

NEW ENGLAND COLLEGES
7¼" X 10", 1015 Pages Paperback
$29.95 Retail
1-59658-504-8

New England is the birthplace of many prestigious universities, and with so many to choose from, picking the right school can be a tough decision. With inside information on over 34 competive Northeastern schools, *New England Colleges* provides the same high-quality information prospective students expect from College Prowler in one all-inclusive, easy-to-use reference.

Schools of the South

Headin' down south? This book will help you find your way to the perfect school!

SCHOOLS OF THE SOUTH
7¼" X 10", 773 Pages Paperback
$29.95 Retail
1-59658-503-X

Southern pride is always strong. Whether it's across town or across state, many Southern students are devoted to their home sweet home. *Schools of the South* offers an honest student perspective on 36 universities available south of the Mason-Dixon.

Untangling
the Ivy League

The ultimate book for everything Ivy!

UNTANGLING THE IVY LEAGUE
7¼" X 10", 567 Pages Paperback
$24.95 Retail
1-59658-500-5

Ivy League students, alumni, admissions officers,
and other top insiders get together to tell it like it is.
Untangling the Ivy League covers every aspect—from
admissions and athletics to secret societies and urban
legends—of the nation's eight oldest, wealthiest, and
most competitive colleges and universities.

Need Help Paying For School?
Apply for our scholarship!

College Prowler awards thousands of dollars a year to students who compose the best essays. E-mail scholarship@collegeprowler.com for more information, or call 1-800-290-2682.

Apply now at **www.collegeprowler.com**

Tell Us What Life Is Really Like at Your School!

Have you ever wanted to let people know what your college is really like? Now's your chance to help millions of high school students choose the right college.

Let your voice be heard.

Check out *www.collegeprowler.com* for more info!

Need More Help?

Do you have more questions about this school?
Can't find a certain statistic? College Prowler is
here to help. We are the best source of college
information out there. We have a network
of thousands of students who can get the latest
information on any school to you ASAP.
E-mail us at info@collegeprowler.com with your
college-related questions.

E-Mail Us Your College-Related Questions!

Check out ***www.collegeprowler.com*** for more details.
1-800-290-2682

Write For Us!
Get published! Voice your opinion.

Writing a College Prowler guidebook is both fun and rewarding; our open-ended format allows your own creativity free reign. Our writers have been featured in national newspapers and have seen their names in bookstores across the country. Now is your chance to break into the publishing industry with one of the country's fastest-growing publishers!

Apply now at *www.collegeprowler.com*

Contact editor@collegeprowler.com or call 1-800-290-2682 for more details.

Pros and Cons

Still can't figure out if this is the right school for you?
You've already read through this in-depth guide; why not
list the pros and cons? It will really help with narrowing down
your decision and determining whether or not
this school is right for you.

Pros	Cons
....	....
....	....
....	....
....	....
....	....
....	....
....	....
....	....
....	....
....	....
....	....
....	....
....	....

Pros and Cons

Still can't figure out if this is the right school for you?
You've already read through this in-depth guide; why not
list the pros and cons? It will really help with narrowing down
your decision and determining whether or not
this school is right for you.

Pros	Cons
....	....
....	....
....	....
....	....
....	....
....	....
....	....
....	....
....	....
....	....
....	....
....	....
....	....

Notes

....

....

....

....

....

....

....

....

....

....

....

....

....

Notes

....
....
....
....
....
....
....
....
....
....
....
....
....

Notes

....

....

....

....

....

....

....

....

....

....

....

....

....

Notes

....

....

....

....

....

....

....

....

....

....

....

....

....

....

Notes

....

....

....

....

....

....

....

....

....

....

....

....

....

Notes

....

....

....

....

....

....

....

....

....

....

....

....

....

Notes

....

....

....

....

....

....

....

....

....

....

....

....

....

Notes

....

....

....

....

....

....

....

....

....

....

....

....

....

....

Notes

....

....

....

....

....

....

....

....

....

....

....

....

....

....

Notes

....

....

....

....

....

....

....

....

....

....

....

....

....

....

Notes

Notes

....
....
....
....
....
....
....
....
....
....
....
....
....